PORTUGUESE
SELF-TAUGHT
(THIMM'S SYSTEM)
WITH
PHONETIC PRONUNCIATION

PORTUGUESE

SELF-TAUGHT

(THIMM'S SYSTEM)

WITH

PHONETIC PRONUNCIATION

E. DA. CUNHA

ISBN : 978-93-5324-599-3 (HB)

First Published, 1904

Published, 2020

Published by

Facsimile Publisher
12 Pragati Market
Ashok Vihar, Ph-2
Delhi-110052
E-mail: books@facsimilepublisher.com

Printed at: G. Print Process, Delhi.

Portuguese Self-Taught
(Thimm's System)
with
Phonetic Pronunciation

Author: E. DA. Cunha

MARLBOROUGH'S SELF-TAUGHT SERIES

Portuguese Self-Taught

(THIMM'S SYSTEM.)

WITH

PHONETIC PRONUNCIATION.

CONTAINING

VOCABULARIES—IDIOMATIC PHRASES AND SENTENCES
ELEMENTARY GRAMMAR
COMMERCIAL, TRADING, LEGAL & RELIGIOUS TERMS
TRAVEL TALK—PHOTOGRAPHY—CYCLING
MOTORING—AMUSEMENTS
&c., &c.

BY

E. da CUNHA.

PHILADELPHIA:
DAVID McKAY COMPANY
PUBLISHERS

PREFACE.

THE addition of this manual of *Portuguese* to "Marlborough's Self-Taught Series" completes the group of modern Latin languages included in the series.

To anyone with a knowledge of *Spanish*, particularly if that knowledge has been obtained through the medium of Marlborough's system of Phonetic Pronunciation, the acquirement of the sister tongue by the aid of PORTUGUESE SELF-TAUGHT will present no difficulty. The most noticeable differences, perhaps, are the absence of the Spanish gutturals, and the unexpected presence of the nasal sound, resembling the French nasal, which is a feature of the Portuguese language though not found in Spanish.

The third or phonetic column, which is added throughout the *Vocabularies* and the *Conversational Phrases and Sentences*, supplies the pronunciation of every word in so simple and natural a manner that the Business man, Tourist, or Traveller is enabled to speak the language intelligibly without previous acquaintance with it, and with the minimum of trouble in mastering the system of phonetics employed. The key to the pronunciation is given in the opening pages of the book, and can be readily referred to for any arbitrary phonetic sign which by its nature is not clearly self-explanatory.

In view of the friendly and important business relations, both political and commercial, so long subsisting between Great Britain on the one hand, and Portugal and the countries of the New World where Portuguese is spoken on the other, this language has not hitherto been sufficiently studied by the British. I trust therefore that this manual will be the means of popularising the acquisition of the language, and that for practical utility, both as a phrase-book for Tourists, Travellers, and Commercial men, and as an introduction to a thorough study of Portuguese, it will be found equal in all respects to the standard of the preceding works of the series.

E. DA CUNHA.

London, 1904.

CONTENTS.

CONTENTS.

PORTUGUESE SELF-TAUGHT.

The Alphabet with Phonetic Pronunciation.

The Portuguese Alphabet has 25 single letters and 6 double consonants:—

Characters.	Name and English Pronunciation.	Phonetics used.
A, a —	(*ah*) has four sounds, viz., (1) When accented* like *a* in *father*, as *fado* [fah'doo]. When followed by a consonant in the same syllable (accented), it is not dwelt on, as in *cavallo* [ke(r)vahl'loo] † ...	a, ah
	(2) In unaccented syllables like *a* in *postman*, *assert*, etc., as *bater* (but-ehr') ...	u, e(r)‡
	(3) When final and not accented, like *a* in *umbrella*, as *fada* [fah'de(r)]	e(r)
	(4) Before *lh* and soft *g*, it is softened to something like the English diphthong *i* (as in *file*) but less distinct; thus *alho* (*i*'l-yoo), *passagem* [pe(r)si'zhen(*g*)]	*i*
B, b —	(*bay*) as in English	b
C, c —	(*say*) may be either hard or soft, viz., Hard before *a*, *o*, *u*, *cl*, and *cr*, as in *casa* [kah'ze(r)], *comida* [koomee'de(r)]	k
	Soft, like *s*, before *e*, *i*, and *y*, as in *cedo* (sai'doo), *cima* [see'me(r)], *cypreste* (see-presh'ti), OR, with cedilla (*ç*), before *a*, *o*, or *u*, as *praça* [prah'se(r)], *môço* (moh'soo), *beiçudo* (baysoo'doo)	s
	[Double *c* (cc) in Portuguese is pronounced as *c*, *cç* as *ç*, and in *ct* the *c* is usually silent]	
D, d —	(*day*) as in English	d

* i.e. when *stress* is laid upon it.

† This remark applies to the other vowels.

‡ The *r* is added to give the *e* the sound of the *e* in *brother*, and it is put in parenthesis to indicate that it must NOT be sounded itself.

Characters.	Name and English Pronunciation.	Phonetics used.
E, e —	(*ai*) has three sounds, viz.,	
	(1) Like *ai* in *paid*, pronounced short and not diphthongised, as *pedra* [paid're(r)] ...	ai
	(2) Something between *e* in *bet* and *e* in *her*, as *pelo* (pel'oo)...	e, eh
	(3) In unaccented syllables, almost like the first *e* in *secure*, as *seguro* (sigoo'roo)... ...	i
	Final *e* is almost as silent as *e* in *vogue*; its sound is between i (short) and e(r) ...	i
F, f —	(*effi*) as in English	f
G, g —	(*zhay*) has two sounds, as in English, viz.,	
	Hard before *a*, *o*, *u*, *l*, and *r*, as *gato* (gah'too)	g, gh
	Soft, like the *s* in *pleasure* before *e* and *i*, as *gelo* (zhel'oo), *gil* (zheel)	zh
H, h —	(*agah'*) is never sounded.	
I, i —	(*ee*) has two sounds, viz.,	
	Long, like *ee* in *feet*, when accented, as *fita* [fee'te(r)]	ee
	Short, like *i* in *if*, when unaccented, as *imprensa* [in(*g*)pren'se(r)]	i
J, j —	[*zhot'e*(*r*)] like *s* in *pleasure*, as *jarro* (zhahr'roo)	zh
K, k —	(*kah*) as in English; only found in words of foreign origin	k
L, l —	(*elli*) as in English	l
M, m—	(*emmi*) as in English	m
	EXCEPT at the end of a syllable or word, when it gives a nasal sound (like na al *n*) to the preceding vowel, as *bom* [boh*n*(*g*)] ...	*n*(*g*)
N, n—	(*enni*) Follows the same rule as *m*, and is pronounced:—	
	(1) As in English	n
	(2) Nasally, as in *anjo* [ah*n*(*g*)'zhoo]... ...	*n*(*g*)

NOTE.—M and N are not nasal before *b*, *p*, *t*, or *d*, as in *onda* [ohn'de(r)].

Characters.	Name and English Pronunciation.	Phonetics used.
O, o —	(*aw*) has three sounds, viz.,	
	(1) Like *aw* in *lawful*, as in *pode* (paw'di) ...	aw
	[In this case the *o* sometimes bears the accent ', as in *cór* (kawr)]	
	(2) Like *o* in *pony*, as *toda* [toh'de(r)] ...	oh*
	[Sometimes marked with the circumflex accent as in *ôvo* (oh'voo)]	
	(3) In unaccented syllables, like *oo*—as in *foot*, NOT as in *boot*—as *todo* (toh'doo) ...	oo
	NOTE.—*Co* and *go* followed by a vowel = *kw* and *gw* respectively, as *lingoado* [lin(*g*)gwah'doo].	
P, p —	(*pay*) as in English	p
Q, q —	(*kay*) like the English *k*, as *qualidade* (kwahleedah'di)	k
	[*Q* is always followed by *u*, which see.]	
R, r —	(*erri*) must always be distinctly sounded, and is rougher than in English at the beginning of a word, and after *l*, *n*, *r*, *s*. Double r (rr) is more strongly pronounced ...	r
S, s —	(*essi*) has four sounds, viz.,	
	(1) Sibilant (*a*) at the beginning of a word, (*b*) after a consonant, (*c*) when double, as *subsistir* (soobsish'teer), *massa* [mah'se(r)] ...	s
	(2) When between two vowels, like the English *z*, as *casa* [kah'ze(r)]	z
	(3) Like *sh*, before *c* (=*k*), *q*, *f*, *ph*, *p*, *s*, *t*, *x*, as *vasto* (vahsh'too)	sh
	(4) Like *s* in *pleasure* before any other consonant, and at the end of a word as *asna* [ahzhne(r)], *fadas* (fah'duzh)	zh
T, t —	(*tay*) as in English	t
U, u —	like *oo* in *food*, but shorter (like *u* in *full*) when unaccented, as *tumulo* (too'mooloo) ...	oo
	When joined to *q*, *u* is silent before *e* and *i*, as *quesito* (kizee'too), *quinta* [keen'te(r)], but before *a* or *o* it is like *u* in *quart*, as *qualidade* [kwahleedah'di), *quota* [kwaw'te(r)]...	w

* A simple sound, not to be diphthongised like *ow* in *owed*.

Characters.	Name and English Pronunciation.	Phonetics used.
V, v —	(*vay*) as in English	v
X, x —	(*sheezh*) is pronounced in four ways, viz.,	
	(1) Like *sh* at the beginning and sometimes in the middle of a word, as *xarope* (shurraw'-pi), *baixo* (bi'shoo)	sh
	(2) Sometimes as *s*, as *proximo* (praw'-simoo)	s
	(3) Sometimes as the English *x*, as *sexo* (sex'oo)...	x
	(4) In *ex* it is like *z* before a vowel, and *sh* before a consonant, as *exemplo* (ez-em'ploo), *expulso* (ishpool'soo)	z, sh
Y, y —	(*ip'silong* or *eegreg'oo*) has two sounds, viz.,	
	Long, like *ee* in *feet*, when accented, as *cysne* (seezh'ni)	ee
	Short when unaccented, as *systema* [sish-tem'e(r)]	i, y
Z, z —	(*zay*) has two sounds, viz.,	
	At the beginning or in the middle of a word, as in English; as *zelo* (zel'oo), *dizer* (deezehr')	z
	At the end of a word, it is like the *z* in *azure*, as *az* (ahzh)	zh

---

The 6 Joint Consonants are as follows:—

Ch, ch –	(1) As a rule, like English *sh*, as *bicho* (bee'shoo)	sh
	(2) In words derived from the Greek pronounced as *k*, as *monarcha* [moonahr'ke(r)]	k
Lh, lh –	is like the *ll* in *billiards*, as *velho* (vel'yoo)	l'y, l-y
Nh, nh –	is like *ny* in *Bunyan*, as *cunha* [koon'ye(r)]	n'y, n-y
Ph, ph –	is like the English *f*, as *philosophia* [filoo-soofee'e(r)]	f
Th, th –	is pronounced as *t*, *theologia* [tiohlohzhee'e(r)]	t
Rh, rh –	is pronounced as *r*, as *rheumatismo* (reh-oo-mahteezh'moo	r

PRELIMINARY NOTES.

Students are recommended to learn the words in the following Vocabularies *by heart*, repeating them aloud with the article attached, aided by the phonetic pronunciation in the third column.

In this way a large number of Portuguese words will be acquired, the gender of the nouns will be mastered, the ear familiarized with the sound of the words, and the tongue with their expression. The same plan should be followed with the phrases and conversations.

The Accents.—There are two accents in the Portuguese language, viz., the acute (′) and the circumflex (^).

The **acute accent** indicates where the stress must be laid, as in *visível* (vizee'vel). It thus distinguishes words spelt alike, e.g.,

Público (poo'blikoo), public; *publico* (poobleek'oo), I publish.
Esta [esh'te(r)], this; *está* (ishtah'), it is.
Da [de(r)], of the; *dá* (dah), gives.

The **circumflex accent** is employed—

(1) To indicate that two vowels coming together are sounded separately, as in *sôa* [soh'e(r)];

(2) To diphthongize a vowel, as in *têa* [teh'i-e(r)], *ôlho* (oil'yoo), &c. (See also letter O, o, page 8.)

Diacritic Signs.—These are as follows:—

(1) The **til** (~) denotes that the vowel over which it is placed is to be sounded *nasally*, as though followed by *m* or *n*, e.g., *lã* [lun(*g*)], *rã* [run(*g*)], *pão* [pown(*g*)].

(2) The **cedilha** (¸) is sometimes placed under c, preceding *a*, *o*, or *u*, to soften it, e.g., *aço* (ah'soo), *pôço* (poh'soo).

Diphthongs.—There are no true diphthongs in Portuguese, each vowel being distinctly sounded; thus *au* is pronounced ah-oo (*or* ow), *ei* is eh-i (ay), *iu* is i-oo (ew), &c.; *ãi* (or *ãe*), *ão* and *õe* are, however, generally described as **nasal diphthongs**, and *ou* is pronounced like *ô* (oh), the *u* being practically silent.

Pronunciation.—This is largely governed by respect for *euphony*. (See S, s, X, x, &c., under *Alphabet*.) The student should make himself familiar with the sounds of the Portuguese letters as given in the preceding pages.

The following points should be noted: In the phonetic columns throughout the book double s (ss) is often used to represent the sibilant, where a single s (s) might be pronounced as z; r is often doubled to ensure its being plainly sounded; occasionally other consonants also are doubled to keep the preceding vowels short; and the hyphen (-) is employed, not to break up a word, but to secure the correct pronunciation of the vowels and consonants. In the third column the accented syllables are indicated as in "oom'e(r)." Unaccented syllables should be pronounced lightly, and not dwelt upon. Examples: *açôr* (ussohr'), *argamasa* [urrgummahs'se(r)], *latido* (lut-ee'doo, *not* lewtee'doo).

Gender.—The gender of each noun in the Vocabularies is indicated either by the article preceding it, or the letter "m." or "f." following it. The masculine articles are: Sing. *o* (the), pl. *os*; *um* (a), *uns* (some); the feminine are: Sing. *a* (the), pl. *as*; *uma* (a), *umas* (some). (See p. 77.)

VOCABULARIES.

1. The World and its Elements.

(O Mundo e seus Elementos.)

(See Notes on ARTICLES, p. 77; GENDER, pp. 77-78.)

English.	Portuguese.	Pronunciation.
The air	*o ar*	oo ahr
the cloud	*a nuvem*	e(r) noo'ven(*g*)
the cold	*o frio*	oo free'oo
the Creator	*o Criador*	oo kree'e(r)dohr
the darkness	*a escuridão*	e(r) ishkooree-down(*g*)'
the dew	*o orvalho*	oo ohrvi'l-yoo
the dust	*a poeira*	e(r) pooay're(r)
the earth	*a terra*	e(r) tair're(r)
East	*Leste, Oriente* m.	lesh'ti, awrien'ti
an eclipse	*um eclipse*	oon(*g*) ekleep'si
the fire	*o fôgo*	oo foh'goo
the fog	*o nevoeiro*	oo nev-ooay'roo
the frost	*a geada*	e(r) zheeah'de(r)
God	*Deus* m.	dai'oozh
the hail	*a saraiva*	e(r) surri've(r)
the heat	*o calor*	oo ke(r)lohr'
Heaven	*Ceo* m.	seh'oo
Hell	*Inferno* m.	een(*g*)fair'noo
the light	*a luz*	e(r) loozh
the lightning	*o relampago*	oo rilump'e(r)goo
the moon	*a lua*	e(r) loo'e(r)
the full moon (new)	*a lua cheia (nova)*	e(r) loo'e(r) shay'e(r) [naw've(r)]
moonlight	*luar* m.	looahr'
nature	*natureza* f.	ne(r)tooreh'ze(r)
North	*Norte* m.	nawr'ti
the rainbow	*o arco-iris*	oo ahr'koo-ee'rizh
the shade, shadow	*a sombra*	e(r) sohm'bre(r)
the sky	*o firmamento*	oo feerme(r)men'too
South	*Sul* m.	sool
the sun	*o sol*	oo sawl
the thunder	*o trovão*	oo troovown(*g*)'
the weather	*o tempo*	oo tem'poo
West	*Oeste, Occidente* m.	ooesh'ti, awsceden'ti
the wind	*o vento*	oo ven'too

2. Land and Water. (*A Terra e a Agua.*)

English.	Portuguese.	Pronunciation.
A bay	*uma bahia*	oom'e(r) be(r)-ee'-e(r)
the beach	*a praia*	e(r) pr*i*'e(r)
the cliff	*o penhasco*	oo pen-yahsh'koo
the coast	*a costa*	e(r) kawsh'te(r)
the current, stream	*a corrente*	e(r) koorren'ti
the ebb	*a vasante*	e(r) vuzzun'ti
the flow (rising tide)	*a enchente*	e(r) i*n*(*g*)shen'ti
the foam	*a espuma*	e(r) ishpoo'me(r)
a hill	*um monte*	oo*n*(*g*) mohn'ti
the ice	*o gelo*	oo zhel'oo
an island	*uma ilha*	oom'e(r) eel'ye(r)
the lake	*o lago*	oo lah'goo
the land	*a terra*	e(r) tair're(r)
the mainland	*o continente*	oo kohnteenen'ti
the mountain	*a montanha*	e(r) mohntun'ye(r)
the mud	*a lama*	e(r) lum'e(r)
a peninsula	*uma peninsula*	oom'e(r) penee*ng*'soole(r)
the rain	*a chuva*	e(r) shoo've(r)
the river	*o rio*	oo ree'oo
a rock	*uma rocha*	oom'e(r) raw'she(r)
the sand	*a areia*	e(r) urray'e(r)
the sea	*o mar*	oo mahr
the shore	*a costa*	e(r) kawsh'te(r)
the snow	*a neve*	e(r) nev'i
a star	*uma estrella*	oom'e(r) ishtrel'le(r)
the storm	*a tempestade*	e(r) tempishtah'di
the stream	*o arroyo*	oo urroy'oo
a thaw	*um degêlo*	oo*n*(*g*) di-zhel'oo
the tide	*a maré*	e(r) murrai'
at high tide	*na preamar*	ne(r) pree-e(r)mahr'
at low tide	*na baixamar*	ne(r) b*i*-she(r)mahr'
a valley	*um valle*	oo*n*(*g*) vahl'li
water, the fresh	*a agua dôce*	e(r) ah'gwe(r) doh'si
—, the salt	*— — salgada*	— — sahlgah'de(r)
a waterfall	*uma cascata*	oom'e(r) kushkah'te(r)
the wave	*a onda*	e(r) ohn'de(r)
a well	*um pôço*	oo*n*(*g*) poh'soo

3. Minerals and Metals. (*Mineraes e Metaes.*)

English.	Portuguese.	Pronunciation.
The agate	*a agata*	e(r) e(r)gah'te(r)
the alum	*a pedra hume*	e(r) paid're(r) oo'mi
the amber	*o ambar*	oo um'burr
the bloodstone	*a hematites*	e(r) em-e(r)tee'tizh
brass	*latão* m.	le(r)town(g)'
bronze	*bronze* m.	brohn(g)'zi
the carbuncle	*o carbunculo*	oo kurrboon(g)'kooloo
cement	*cimento* m.	seement'oo
the chalk	*o giz*	oo zheezh
clay	*barro* m.	bahr'roo
the coal	*o carvão de pedra*	oo kurrvown(g)' di paid're(r)
the copper	*o cobre*	oo kaw'bri
the coral	*o coral*	oo koorahl'
the crystal	*o crystal*	oo kreeshtahl'
the diamond	*o diamante*	oo dee-e(r)mun'ti
the emerald	*a esmeralda*	e(r) izhmerrahl'de(r)
the glass	*o vidro*	oo veed'roo
the gold	*o ouro*	oo oh'roo
granite	*granito* m.	grun'itoo
the gravel	*o cascalho*	oo ke(r)shki'l-yoo
the iron	*o ferro*	oo fair'roo
iron, the cast	— — *fundido*	— — foondee'doo
—, the wrought	— — *forjado*	— — foorzhah'doo
lead	*chumbo* m.	shoom'boo
the lime	*a cal*	e(r) kahl
the marble	*o marmore*	oo mahr'moori
mercury	*mercurio* m.	merrkoo'reeoo
the metals	*os metaes*	oozh mitti'zh
mortar	*argamassa* f.	urrgummahs'se(r)
an opal	*uma opala*	oom'e(r) ohpahl'e(r)
the pearl	*a perola*	e(r) pair'oole(r)
a ruby	*um rubim*	oon(g) roobeen(g)'
the sapphire	*a saphira*	e(r) se(r)fee're(r)
the silver	*a prata*	e(r) prah'te(r)
soda	*soda* f.	saw'de(r)
the steel	*o aço*	oo ah'soo
the stone	*a pedra*	e(r) paid're(r)
the tin	*o estanho*	oo ishtun'yoo

4. Animals, Birds and Fishes.

(*Animaes, Aves e Peixes.*)

English.	Portuguese.	Pronunciation.
An animal	*um animal*	oo*n*(*g*) un-eemahl'
the barking	*o latido*	oo lut-ee'doo
a bear	*um urso*	oo*n*(*g*) oor'soo
a bird	*um passaro*	oo*n*(*g*) pahs'surroo
a blackbird	*um melro*	oo*n*(*g*) mel'roo
bleating	*balido* m.	be(r)lee'doo
braying	*zurrido* m.	zoorree'doo
a bull	*um touro*	oo*n*(*g*) toh'roo
a calf	*um bezerro*	oo*n*(*g*) bizair'roo
a carp	*uma carpa*	oom'e(r) kahr'pe(r)
the cat	*o gato*	oo gah'too
the cattle	*o gado*	oo gah'doo
a chicken	*um frango*	oo*n*(*g*) fru*n*(*g*)'goo
the claw	*a garra*	e(r) gahr're(r)
a cock	*um gallo*	oo*n*(*g*) gahl'loo
a cod	*um bacalhao*	oo*n*(*g*) buk-ul-yow'
the colt	*o potro*	oo poh'troo
a cow	*uma vacca*	oom'e(r) vahk'ke(r)
a crab	*um caranguejo*	oo*n*(*g*) kurru*n*(*g*)gai'zhoo
the crow	*o corvo*	oo kohr'voo
a cuckoo	*um cucu*	oo*n*(*g*) koo'koo
the dog	*o cão*	oo kow*n*(*g*)
a donkey	*um burro*	oo*n*(*g*) boor'roo
the dove	*a rola*	e(r) rohl'e(r)
a duck	*um pato*	oo*n*(*g*) pah'too
duck, a wild	— — *bravo*	— — brah'voo
the eagle	*a aguia*	e(r) ah'ghee-e(r)
an eel	*uma enguia*	oom'e(r) i*n*(*g*)ghee'e(r)
an elephant	*um elephante*	oo*n*(*g*) illifun'ti
a feather	*uma penna*	oom'e(r) pen'ne(r)
the fins	*as barbatanas*	uzh burrbut-un'uzh
a fish	*um peixe*	oo*n*(*g*) pay'shi
the fox	*a raposa*	e(r) re(r)poh'ze(r)
the fur	*o pello*	oo pel'loo
the gills	*as guelras*	uzh ghel'ruzh
a he-goat	*um bode*	oo*n*(*g*) baw'di
a she-goat	*uma cabra*	oom'e(r) kah'bre(r)

English.	Portuguese.	Pronunciation.
a goose	*um ganso*	oo*n*(*g*) gu*n*(*g*)'soo
grouse	*gallo* (m.) *das urzes*	gahl'loo duz oor'zizh
a gull	*uma gaivota*	oom'e(r) gh*i*-vaw'te(r)
the hair	*o cabello*	oo ke(r)bel'loo
the hare	*a lebre*	e(r) leb'ri
a hawk	*um açôr*	oo*n*(*g*) ussohr'
a hen	*uma gallinha*	oom'e(r) gulleen'ye(r)
the herd	*a manada*	e(r) mun-ah'de(r)
a herring	*um arenque*	oo*n*(*g*) urre*n*(*g*)'ki
the hoof	*o casco*	oo kahsh'koo
the horn	*o chifre*	oo shee'fri
a horse	*um cavallo*	oo*n*(*g*) ke(r)vahl'loo
howling	*huivar* (verb)	oo-eevahr'
a lamb	*um cordeiro*	oo*n*(*g*) koorday'roo
a lark	*uma calhandra*	oom'e(r) kul-yun'dre(r)
a lion	*um leão*	oo*n*(*g*) li-ow*n*(*g*)'
a lobster	*uma lagôsta*	oom'e(r) le(r)gohsh'te(r)
a mackerel	*uma sarda*	oom'e(r) sahr'de(r)
a magpie	*uma pêga*	oom'e(r) peg'e(r)
the mane	*a crina*	e(r) kree'ne(r)
a mole	*uma toupeira*	oom'e(r) tohpay're(r)
a monkey	*um macaco*	oo*n*(*g*) me(r)kah'koo
the mouse	*o rato*	oo rah'too
a mule	*uma mula*	oom'e(r) mool'e(r)
a nightingale	*um rouxinol*	oo*n*(*g*) rohsheenawl'
an owl	*um môcho*	oo*n*(*g*) moh'shoo
an ox	*um boi*	oo*n*(*g*) boy
oysters	*ostras* f.pl.	awsh'truzh
the parrot	*o papagaio*	oo pe(r)pe(r)gh*i*'oo
a partridge	*uma perdiz*	oom'e(r) perrdeezh'
the paw	*a pata*	e(r) pah'te(r)
the pheasant	*o faisão*	oo fi-zow*n*(*g*)'
a pig	*um pôrco*	oo*n*(*g*) pohr'koo
a pigeon	*uma pomba*	oom'e(r) pohm'be(r)
a pike	*um lucio*	oo*n*(*g*) loo'sioo
a quail	*uma codorniz*	oom'e(r) koodoorneezh'
the rat	*a ratazana*	e(r) rut-uz-un'e(r)
the raven	*o côrvo*	oo kohr'voo
a salmon	*um salmão*	oo*n*(*g*) sahlmow*n*(*g*)'
salt fish	*peixe* (m.) *salgado*	pay'shi sahlgah'doo

English.	Portuguese.	Pronunciation.
the scales	*as escamas*	uzh ishkum'uzh
a seal	*uma phoca*	oom'e(r) faw'ke(r)
a sheep	*um carneiro*	oo*n*(*g*) kurrnay'roo
the snipe	*a narseja*	e(r) nurrsay'zhe(r)
a sole	*um linguado*	oo*n*(*g*) li*n*(*g*)gwah'doo
the sparrow	*o pardal*	oo purrdahl'
the swallow	*a andorinha*	e(r) undoo-reen'ye(r)
a swan	*um cysne*	oo*n*(*g*) seezh'ni
the tail	*o rabo*	oo rah'boo
a thrush	*um tôrdo*	oo*n*(*g*) tohr'doo
a tiger	*um tigre*	oo*n*(*g*) tee'gri
a trout	*uma truta*	oom'e(r) troo'te(r)
a turbot	*um rodovalho*	oo*n*(*g*) roodoovi'l-yoo
a turkey	*um perú*	oo*n*(*g*) piroo'
a turtle	*uma tartaruga*	oom'e(r) turturroo'ghe(r)
a whale	*uma baleia*	oom'e(r) be(r)lay'e(r)
a whiting	*uma pescadinha*	oom'e(r) pishke(r)deen'ye(r)
a wing	*uma aza*	oom'e(r) ah'ze(r)
the wolf	*o lôbo*	oo loh'boo
a woodpecker	*um pica pau*	oo*n*(*g*) peek'e(r) pow
a wood-pigeon	*um pombo silvestre*	oo*n*(*g*) pohm'boo silvesh'tri

5. Reptiles and Insects. (*Reptis e Insectos.*)

English.	Portuguese.	Pronunciation.
An ant	*uma formiga*	oom'e(r) foormee'ghe(r)
a bee	*uma abelha*	oom'e(r) e(r)bel'ye(r)
a beetle	*uma barata*	oom'e(r) burrah'te(r)
a bug	*um persevejo*	oo*n*(*g*) perrsivay'zhoo
a butterfly	*uma borboleta*	oom'e(r) boorboolet'e(r)
a caterpillar	*uma lagarta*	oom'e(r) lug-ahr'te(r)
a flea	*uma pulga*	oom'e(r) pool'ghe(r)
a fly	*uma mosca*	oom'e(r) mohsh'ke(r)
a frog	*uma rã*	oom'e(r) ru*n*(*g*)
a gnat	*um mosquito*	oo*n*(*g*) mooshkee'too
the grasshopper	*a cigarra*	e(r) sigahr're(r)
an insect	*um insecto*	oo*n*(*g*) ee*n*(*g*)sek'too
the lizard	*a lagartixa*	e(r) le(r)gurrtee'she(r)
a mosquito	*um mosquito*	oo*n*(*g*) mooshkee'too
a moth	*uma maripousa*	oom'e(r) murripoh'se(r)

English.	Portuguese.	Pronunciation.
the serpent	*a serpente*	e(r) serrpen'ti
a silkworm	*um bicho de sêda*	oon(g) bee'shoo di sed'e(r)
a snail	*um caracol*	oon(g) kurre(r)kawl'
a snake	*uma cobra*	oom'e(r) kaw'bre(r)
a spider	*uma aranha*	oom'e(r) urrun'ye(r)
a sting	*um ferrão*	oon(g) ferrown(g)'
a toad	*um sapo*	oon(g) sah'poo
a viper	*uma vibora*	oom'e(r) vee'boore(r)
a wasp	*uma vêspa*	oom'e(r) vesh'pe(r)
a worm	*um bicho*	oon(g) bee'shoo

6. Fruits, Trees, Flowers, and Vegetables.

(Frutas, Arvores, Flôres e Hortaliças.)

(See Shopping, p. 109.)

An apple	*uma maçã*	oom'e(r) mussun(g)'
an apricot	*um damasco*	oong de(r)mahsh'koo
an ash	*um freixo*	oon(g) fray'shoo
the asparagus	*os espargos*	ooz ishpahr'goozh
the bark	*a casca*	e(r) kahsh'ke(r)
the beans	*as favas*	uzh fah'vuzh
beans, the French	*o feijão carrapato*	oo fayzhown(g)' kurre(r)-
the beech-tree	*a faia*	e(r) fi'e(r) [pah'too
the beetroot	*a beterraba*	e(r) bitterrah'be(r)
the birch	*a bétula*	e(r) bai'toole(r) [ve(r)
the blackberry	*a amora de silva*	e(r) um-aw're(r) di seel'-
a bouquet	*um ramalhete*	oon(g) rum-ul-yet'i
a branch	*um ramo*	oon(g) rum'oo
— — (cut-off)	*— — cortado*	— — koortah'doo
the cabbage	*a couve*	e(r) koh'vi
the carrot	*a cenoura*	e(r) sinoh're(r)
the cauliflower	*a couve-flôr*	e(r) koh'vi-flohr
the celery	*o aipo*	oo i'poo
a cherry	*uma cerêja*	oom'e(r) si-ray'zhe(r)
a chestnut	*uma castanha*	oom'e(r) kushtun'ye(r)
cinnamon	*canella* f.	kun-el'le(r)
the cucumber	*o pepino*	oo pipeen'oo
currant, the black	*a groselha preta*	e(r) groozel'ye(r) pret'e(r)
—, the red	*— — vermelha*	— — verrmel'ye(r)
—, the white	*— — branca*	— — brun(g)'ke(r)

English.	Portuguese.	Pronunciation.
the fagot	*o molho de lenha*	oo mohl'yoo di len'ye(r)
a fig	*um figo*	oo*n*(*g*) fee'goo
the fig-tree	*a figueira*	e(r) feeghay're(r)
a filbert	*uma avellã*	oom'e(r) uvve(r)llu*n*(*g*)'
the fir-tree	*o pinheiro manso*	oo pinyay'roo mu*n*(*g*)'soo
a flower	*uma flôr*	oom'e(r) flohr'
the garlic	*o alho*	oo *i*'l-yoo
the gherkins	*os pepinos de conserva*	oozh pipeen'oozh di koh*n*(*g*)sair've(r)
ginger	*gengibre* m.	zhe*n*(*g*)zhee'bri
a gooseberry	*uma uva crespa*	oom'e(r) oo've(r) kresh'pe(r)
the grapes	*as uvas*	uz oo'vuzh
the ivy	*a hera*	e(r) eh'rah
the kernel	*o carôço*	oo kurroh'soo
a leaf	*uma folha*	oom'e(r) fohl'ye(r)
a lemon	*um limão*	oo*n*(*g*) leemow*n*(*g*)'
the lettuce	*a alface*	e(r) ahlfah'si
a lily	*um lirio*	oo*n*(*g*) lee'reeoo
the lily-of-the-valley	*o lirio do valle*	oo lee'reeoo doo vahl'li
a lime	*uma lima*	oom'e(r) lee'me(r)
mace	*maciz* m.	musseezh'
a melon	*um melão*	oo*n*(*g*) melow*n*(*g*)'
a mulberry	*uma amora*	oom'e(r) um-aw're(r)
myrtle	*murta* f.	moor'te(r)
a nettle	*uma urtiga*	oom'e(r) oortee'ghe(r)
a nut	*uma noz*	oom'e(r) nawzh
the oak-tree	*o carvalho*	oo kurrv*i*'l-yoo
an olive	*uma azeitona*	oom'e(r) e(r)zaytoh'ne(r)
a peach	*um pecego*	oo*n*(*g*) pess'igoo
a pear	*uma pêra*	oom'e(r) pai're(r)
peas (green)	*ervilhas verdes*	ehr-veel'yuzh vair'dizh
a pine (tree)	*um pinheiro bravo*	oo*n*(*g*) peen-yay'roo brah'voo
the pine-apple	*o ananaz*	oo un-un-ahzh'
a pink	*um cravo*	oo*n*(*g*) krah'voo
a plum	*uma ameixa*	oom'e(r) um-aish'e(r)
potatoes	*batatas* f.	but-ah'tuzh
the radishes	*os rabanos*	oozh rah'bun-oozh
a raspberry	*uma framboeza*	oom'e(r) frumboo-ez'e(r)
the root	*a raiz*	e(r) re(r)-eezh'
a rose	*uma rosa*	oom'e(r) raw'ze(r)

English.	Portuguese.	Pronunciation.
the spinach	*os espinafres*	ooz ishpeenah'frizh
the stalk (of plant)	*a hastea*	e(r) ahsh'tee-e(r)
a strawberry	*um morango*	oon(*g*) moorun(*g*)'goo
the stump (of a tree)	*o cêpo*	oo sai'poo
a tomato	*um tomate*	oon(*g*) toomah'ti
a tree	*uma arvore*	oom'e(r) ahr'voori
a tree-trunk	*um tronco d'uma arvore*	oon(*g*) troh'n(*g*)koo d'oom'e(r) ahr'voori
a tulip	*uma tulipa*	oom'e(r) too'lipe(r)
a turnip	*um nabo*	oon(*g*) nah'boo
the vine	*a vinha*	e(r) veen'ye(r)
a violet	*uma violeta*	oom'e(r) veeoolet'e(r)
a walnut	*uma noz*	oom'e(r) nawzh
the watercress	*o agreão*	oo e(r)greeown(*g*)'
the wax	*a cêra*	e(r) sai're(r)
the willow	*o salgueiro*	oo sahlgay'roo

7. Colours.* (*Côres.*)

English.	Portuguese.	Pronunciation.
Black	*preto* m., *preta* f.	pret'oo, pret'e(r)
blue; navy blue	*azul; — marinho*	uz-ool'; — murreen'yoo
brown	*castanho, -a*	kushtun'yoo, -ye(r)
crimson	*carmezim*	kurrmi-zeen(*g*)'
dark	*escuro, -a*	ishkoo'roo, -e(r)
deep	*carregado, -a*	kurrigah'doo, -e(r)
fawn	*pardo, -a*	pahr'doo, -e(r)
green	*verde*	vair'di
grey	*cinzento, -a*	seen(*g*)zen'too, -e(r)
light (pale)	*claro, -a (pallido, -a)*	klah'roo, -er (pahl'leeldoo, -e(r))
lilac	*lilaz*	leelahzh'
orange	*laranjado, -a*	lurrun(*g*)zhah'doo, -e(r)
pink	*rosado, -a*	rawzah'doo, -e(r)
purple	*rôxo, -a*	roh'shoo, -e(r)
red	*encarnado, -a*	in(*g*)kurnah'doo, -e(r)
scarlet	*escarlate*	ishkurrlah'ti
violet	*violete*	veeoolet'i
white	*branco, -a*	brun(*g*)'koo, -e(r)
yellow	*amarello, -a*	ummurrel'loo, -e(r)

* The words in this list are adjectives, some of which have different terminations for masculine and feminine, as *pret-o* m., *pret-a* f.; others only one for both, as *verde* m. & f.

8. Times and Seasons. *(Epocas e Estações.)*

(For Conversations see page 106.)

English.	Portuguese.	Pronunciation.
The afternoon	*a tarde*	e(r) tahr'di
the birthday	*o dia d'annos*	oo dee'e(r) d'un'noozh
Christmas	*Natal* m.	nut-ahl'
— Eve	*Vesperas do Natal*	vesh'peruzh doo nut-ahl'
the dawn	*o amanhecer*	oo um-un-yeh-sair'
the day	*o dia*	oo dee'e(r)
day, to-	*hoje*	oy'zhi
days of the week	*dias da semana*	dee'uzh de(r) si-mun'e(r)
Monday	*Segunda feira*	sigoon'de(r) fay're(r)
Tuesday	*Terça feira*	tair'se(r) fay're(r)
Wednesday	*Quarta feira*	kwahr'te(r) fay're(r)
Thursday	*Quinta feira*	keen'te(r) fay're(r)
Friday	*Sexta feira*	sesh'te(r) fay're(r)
Saturday	*Sabbado*	sahb'bud-oo
Sunday	*Domingo*	doomee*n*(*g*)'goo
dusk	*crepusculo* m.	kripoosh'kooloo
Easter	*a Pascoa*	e(r) pahsh'koo-e(r)
the eve	*as vesperas*	uzh vesh'peruzh
evening	*á noitinha*	ah noyteen'ye(r)
a fortnight	*uma quinzena*	oom'e(r) kee*n*(*g*)zen'e(r)
Good-Friday	*Sexta-feira Santa*	sesh'te(r) - fay're(r) sunt'e(r)
a holiday	*um dia feriado*	[doo oo*n*(*g*) dee'e(r) ferreeah'-doo
Holy Week	*a Semana Santa*	e(r) si-mun'e(r) sunt'e(r)
an hour	*uma hora*	oom'e(r) aw're(r)
— —, half-	*meia hora*	may'e(r) aw're(r)
Lent	*a Quaresma*	e(r) kwurrezh'me(r)
Michaelmas	*Dia de São Miguel*	dee'e(r) di sow*n*(*g*) mee-ghel'
mid-day	*meio dia*	may'oo dee'e(r)
midnight	*meia noite*	may'e(r) noy'ti
Midsummer	*Estio* m.	ishtee'oo
the minute	*o minuto*	oo meenoo'too
a month	*um mez*	oo*n*(*g*) mezh
month, last	*o mez proximo passado*	oo mezh praw'simoo pus-sah'doo
—, next	*— — — futuro*	— — — foo-too'roo

English.	Portuguese.	Pronunciation.
months, the	*os mezes*	oozh mez'ezh
January	*Janeiro*	zhun-ay'roo
February	*Fevereiro*	fev-i-ray'roo
March	*Março*	mahr'soo
April	*Abril*	e(r)breel'
May	*Maio*	mi'oo
June	*Junho*	zhoon'yoo
July	*Julho*	zhool'yoo
August	*Agosto*	e(r)gohsh'too
September	*Setembro*	sitem'broo
October	*Outubro*	ohtoo'broo
November	*Novembro*	noovem'broo
December	*Dezembro*	di-zem'broo
morning, the	*a manhã*	e(r) mun-yun(g)'
to-morrow	*ámanhã*	ahmun-yun(g)'
the night	*a noite*	e(r) noy'ti
noon	*meio dia*	may'oo dee'e(r)
a quarter	*um quarto*	oon(g) kwahr'too
— — of an hour	*— — de hora*	— — di aw're(r)
the season (time of year)	*a estação (epoca do anno)*	e(r) ishtussown(g)' (ep'ooke(r) doo un'noo)
the seasons	*as estações*	uz ishtussoy'n(g)zh
Spring	*Primavera*	preeme(r)vai're(r)
Summer	*Verão*	verrown(g)'
Autumn	*Outono*	ohtoh'noo
Winter	*Inverno*	een(g)vair'noo
a second	*um segundo*	oon(g) sigoon'doo
sunrise	*o nascer do sol*	oo nuzh-sair' doo sawl
sunset	*o pôr do sol*	oo pohr doo sawl
time	*a hora*	e(r) aw're(r)
	tempo	tem'poo
twilight	*crepusculo*	kripoosh'kooloo
a week	*uma semana*	oom'e(r) si-mun'e(r)
week-day	*dia de semana*	dee'e(r) di si-mun'e(r)
weekly	*semanalmente*	simmun-ahlmen'ti
Whitsuntide	*Pentecoste*	pentikawsh'ti
a year	*um anno*	oon(g) un'noo
yesterday	*hontem*	ohn'ten(g)
— morning	*— de manhã*	— di mun-yun(g)'
— evening	*— á noite*	— ah noy'ti

9. Public Holidays in Portugal.

(Dias de Festa em Portugal.)

English.	Portuguese.	Pronunciation.
New Year's Day	*Dia de Anno Bom*	dee'e(r) di un'noo bohn(g)
Epiphany	*Epiphania*	ip-eefun-ee'e(r) [te(r)
Holy Thursday	*Quinta feira Santa*	keen'te(r) fay're(r) sun'-
Good Friday	*Sexta feira Santa*	sesh'te(r) fay're(r) sun'-
		te(r) [zay'
Feast of St. Joseph	*Festa de São José*	fesh'te(r) di sown(g) zhoo-
Ascension Day	*Dia da Ascensão*	dee'e(r) de(r) us-sen(g)-
	[Deos	sown(g)' [day'oozh
Corpus Christi	*Dia de Corpo de*	dee'er di kohr'poo di
The Assumption	*A Assumpção*	e(r) us-soon(g)-sown(g)'
Feast of St. Peter	*Festa de São Pedro*	fesh'te(r) di sown(g) ped'-
The Carnival	*O Carnaval*	oo kurrne(r)vahl' [roo
All Saints' Day	*Dia de todos os Santos*	dee'e(r) di toh'doozh ooz sun'toozh
The Immaculate Conception	*A Santissima Concepção*	e(r) suntees'sime(r) kon(g)saisown(g)'
Christmas	*Natal*	nut-ahl'

10. Town and Country. *(A Cidade e o Campo.)*

(For Conversations see page 107.)

A bank (mound)	*um outeiro*	oon(g) ohtay'roo
the barn	*o celleiro*	oo sellay'roo
the bridge	*a ponte*	e(r) pohn'ti
the brook	*o ribeiro*	oo reebay'roo
a building (edifice)	*um edificio*	oon(g) idifee'sioo
the bush	*o arbusto*	oo ahrboosh'too
the cathedral	*a cathedral*	e(r) ke(r)ted'rahl
a church	*uma igreja*	oom'e(r) igray'zhe(r)
the country	*o campo*	oo kum'poo
the courtyard	*o patio*	oo pah'tioo
the dale	*o valle*	oo vahl'li
a ditch	*um fosso*	oon(g) faws'soo
a farm	*uma herdade*	oom'e(r) errdah'di
a fence	*um tapume*	oon(g) te(r)poo'mi
the field	*o campo*	oo kum'poo
a foot-path	*um caminho*	oon(g) kummeen'yoo
the forest	*a floresta*	e(r) floo-resh'te(r)

English.	Portuguese.	Pronunciation.
the gate (little)	*a cancella*	e(r) kun(*g*)sel'le(r)
— — (large)	*o portão*	oo poortown(*g*)
the grass	*a relva*	e(r) rel've(r)
the hay	*o feno*	oo fen'oo
the hay-stack	*a pilha de feno*	e(r) peel'ye(r) di fen'oo
the hedge	*a sebe*	e(r) seb'i
the high-road	*a estrada real*	e(r) ishtrah'de(r) reeahl'
a hospital	*um hospital*	oo*n*(*g*) ooshpitahl'
the huntsman	*o caçador*	oo kusse(r)dohr'
the hut	*a choupana*	e(r) shoh-pun'e(r)
the inn	*a estalagem*	er ishtul-ï'zhe*n*(*g*)
the lane	*a azinhaga*	e(r) e(r)zin-yah'ghe(r)
a log	*um cêpo*	oo*n*(*g*) seh'poo
the market	*o mercado*	oo merrkah'doo
the meadow	*o prado*	oo prah'doo
a mile	*uma milha*	oom'e(r) meel'ye(r)
the mill	*o moinho*	oo mooeen'yoo
a monument	*um monumento*	oo*n*(*g*) mohnooment'oo
the palace	*o palacio*	oo pe(r)lah'sioo
the police-office	*a repartição de policia*	e(r) ripurrtissow*n*(*g*)' di poolee'si-e(r)
the prison	*a cadeia*	e(r) ke(r)day'e(r)
the river	*o rio*	oo ree'oo
the road	*o caminho*	oo kummeen'yoo
the school	*a escola*	e(r) ishkaw'le(r)
the shepherd	*o pastôr*	oo pe(r)shtohr'
a shop	*uma loja*	oom'e(r) law'zhe(r)
the sign-post	*o guião de caminho*	oo ghi-ow*n*(*g*)' di ke(r)-meen'yoo
the soil	*o solo*	oo saw'loo
a square	*uma praça*	oom'e(r) prah'se(r)
the street	*a rua*	e(r) roo'e(r)
the timber	*a madeira*	e(r) me(r)day're(r)
the tower	*a torre*	e(r) tohr'ri
the town	*a villa*	e(r) veel'le(r)
the town-hall	*a casa da camara*	e(r) kah'ze(r) de(r) kum'-urre(r).
the university	*a universidade*	e(r) ooneeverrsidah'di
the valley	*o valle*	oo vahl'li
the village	*a aldeia*	e(r) ahlday'e(r)
the waterfall	*a cascata*	e(r) ke(r)shkah'te(r)
the wood	*o bosque*	oo bawsh'ki

11. Mankind: Relations.

(O Genero Humano: os Parentes.)

English.	Portuguese.	Pronunciation.
The aunt	*a tia*	e(r) tee'e(r)
a bachelor	*um solteiro*	oon(g) sawltay'roo
a boy	*um rapaz*	oon(g) rup-ahzh'
a bride	*uma noiva*	oom'e(r) noy've(r)
a bridegroom	*um noivo*	oon(g) noy'voo
a brother	*um irmão*	oon(g) eermown(g)'
a brother-in-law	*um cunhado*	oon(g) koon-yah'doo
the child	*a criança*	e(r) kree-un(g)'se(r)
the cousin	*o primo, a prima*	oo preem'oo, e(r) preem'e(r)
the daughter	*a filha*	e(r) feel'ye(r)
the daughter-in-law	*a nora*	e(r) naw're(r)
the family	*a familia*	e(r) fe(r)meel'ye(r)
a father	*um pae*	oon(g) pi
a father-in-law	*um sôgro*	oon(g) soh'groo
a gentleman	*um cavalheiro*	oon(g) kuvvul-yay'roo
a girl	*uma rapariga*	oom'e(r) ruppurree'ghe(r)
a granddaughter	*uma neta*	oom'e(r) net'e(r)
a grandfather	*um avô*	oon(g) e(r)voh'
a grandmother	*uma avó*	oom'e(r) e(r)vaw
a grandson	*um neto*	oon(g) net'oo
the guardian	*o tutor*	oo tootohr'
the heir	*o herdeiro*	oo airday'roo
a husband	*um marido*	oon(g) murree'doo
a lady	*uma dama*	oom'e(r) dum'e(r)
a man	*um homem*	oon(g) aw'men(g)
the marriage	*o casamento*	oo kuzze(r)men'too
a mother	*uma mãe*	oom'e(r) main(g)
a mother-in-law	*uma sogra*	oom'e(r) saw'gre(r)
the nephew	*o sobrinho*	oo soobreen'yoo
the niece	*a sobrinha*	e(r) soobreen'ye(r)
the nobleman	*o fidalgo*	oo feedahl'goo
the nurse	*a ama*	e(r) um'e(r)
the orphan	*o (a) orphão*	oo [e(r)] awrfown(g)'
the parents	*os paes*	oozh pi'zh
the relations	*os parentes*	oozh purren'tizh
the sister	*a irmã*	e(r) eermun(g)'
the sister-in-law	*a cunhada*	e(r) koon-yah'de(r)

English.	Portuguese.	Pronunciation.
the son	*o filho*	oo feel'yoo
the son-in-law	*o genro*	oo zhe*n*(*g*)'roo
a spinster	*uma solteira*	oom'e(r) sawltay're(r)
the uncle	*o tio*	oo tee'oo
the ward	*o pupillo, a pupilla*	oo poopeel'loo, e(r) poopeel'le(r)
the widow	*a viuva*	e(r) vioo've(r)
the widower	*o viuvo*	oo vioo'voo
the wife	*a esposa*	e(r) ishpoh'ze(r)
a woman	*uma mulher*	oom'e(r) mool'yair

12. The Human Body. (*O Corpo Humano.*)

English.	Portuguese.	Pronunciation.
The ankle	*o tornozello*	oo toornoozel'loo
the arm	*o braço*	oo brah'soo
the back	*as costas*	uzh kawsh'tuzh
the beard	*a barba*	e(r) bahr'be(r)
the blood	*o sangue*	oo su*n*(*g*)'ghi
the body	*o corpo*	oo kohr'poo
the bones	*os ossos*	ooz aws'soozh
the bowels	*as visceras*	uzh vee'seruzh
the brain	*o cerebro*	oo sair'ibroo
the breast, chest	*o peito*	oo pay'too
the cheek	*a face*	e(r) fah'si
the chin	*o queixo*	oo kay'shoo
the complexion	*a tez*	e(r) tezh
the ears (internal)	*os ouvidos*	ooz ohvee'doozh
— — (external)	*as orelhas*	uz ohrel'yuzh
the elbow	*o cotovêllo*	oo kootoovel'loo
the eye	*o ôlho*	oo oil'yoo
the eyebrows	*as sobrancelhas*	uzh soobru*n*(*g*)sel'yuzh
the eyelids	*as palpebras*	uzh pahlpeb'ruzh
the eyelashes	*as pestanas*	uzh pishtun'uzh
the face	*a cara*	e(r) kah're(r)
the fingers	*os dedos*	oozh deh'doozh
the foot	*o pé*	oo pay
the forehead	*a testa*	e(r) tesh'te(r)
the groin	*a virilha*	e(r) veereel'ye(r)
the hair	*a cabello*	oo ke(r)bel'loo
the hand	*a mão*	e(r) mow*n*(*g*)
the head	*a cabeça*	e(r) ke(r)bes'se(r)
the heart	*o coração*	oo koore(r)sow*n*(*g*)'

English.	Portuguese.	Pronunciation.
the **heel**	*o calcanhar*	oo kahlkun-yahr'
the hip	*o quadril*	oo kwah'dreel
the jaw	*a queixada*	e(r) kayshah'de(r)
the kidneys	*os rins*	oozh reen(g)zh
the knee	*o joelho*	oo zhooel'yoo
the leg	*a perna*	e(r) pair'ne(r)
the limb	*o membro*	oo mem'broo
the lips	*os beiços*	oozh bay'soozh
the liver	*o figado*	oo fee'ge(r)doo
the lung	*o pulmão*	oo poolmown(g)'
the moustache	*o bigóde*	oo beegaw'di
the mouth	*a bôcca*	e(r) bohk'ke(r)
the nails	*as unhas*	uz oon'yuzh
the neck	*o pescoço*	oo pishkoh'soo
the nose	*o nariz*	oo nurreezh'
the ribs	*as costellas*	uzh kooshtel'luzh
the shoulders	*os hombros*	ooz ohm'broozh
the side	*a ilharga*	e(r) eel-yahr'ghe(r)
the skin	*a pelle*	e(r) pel'li
the skull	*o craneo*	oo krun'ioo
the spine	*o espinhaço*	oo ishpeen-yah'soo
the stomach	*o estomago*	oo ishtoh'me(r)goo
the temple	*a fonte*	e(r) fohn'ti
the throat	*a garganta*	e(r) gurrgun'te(r)
the thumb	*o dedo pollegar*	oo deh'doo pohlligahr'
the toe	*a dedo do pé*	— — doo pay
the tongue	*a lingua*	e(r) leen(g)'gooe(r)
the tooth	*o dente*	oo den'ti
the wrist	*o pulso*	oo pool'soo

13. Health. *(A Saúde.)*

(For Conversations see page 106.)

An accident	*um desastre*	oon(g) dizahsh'tri
the ambulance	*a ambulancia*	e(r) umboolun(g)'si-e(r)
a bandage	*uma atadura*	oom'e(r) utte(r)doo're(r)
biliousness	*bilis* f.	bee'lizh
a bite	*uma mordedura*	oom'e(r) moordidoo're(r)
the blindness	*a cegueira*	e(r) sigay're(r)
a blister	*uma empola*	oom'e(r) em'poole(r)
a bruise	*uma contusão*	oom'e(r) kohntoozown(g)'

English.	Portuguese.	Pronunciation.
a burn	*uma queimadura*	oom'e(r) kaymud-oo're(r)
to catch a complaint	*apanhar uma molestia*	up-un-yahr' oom'e(r) moo-lesh'ti-e(r)
contagion	*contagio* m.	kohntah'zhioo
the chemist's shop	*a pharmacia*	e(r) furrmah'si-e(r)
a chill	*um resfriado*	oo*n*(*g*) rishfriah'doo
to catch a chill	*apanhar um resfriado*	up-un-yahr' oo*n*(*g*) rish-friah'doo
chilblains	*frieiras* f.pl.	free-ay'ruzh
the cough	*a tosse*	e(r) taws'si
the corns	*os callos*	oozh kahl'loozh
cramp	*cambra* f.	kum'bre(r)
a cure	*uma cura*	oom'e(r) koo're(r)
deaf	*surdo, -a*	soor'doo, -e(r)
the dentist	*o dentista*	oo denteesh'te(r)
the diarrhœa	*a diarrhea*	e(r) dee-urray'e(r)
the diet	*a dieta*	e(r) dee-et'e(r)
the disease, illness	*a doença*	e(r) doo-e*n*(*g*)'se(r)
the doctor	*o medico*	oo med'ikoo
the draught	*a poção*	e(r) poosow*n*(*g*)'
dumb	*mudo, -a*	moo'doo, moo'de(r)
exercise	*exercicio* m.	ezzerrsee'sioo
exhaustion	*esfalfamento* m.	ishfahlfe(r)men'too
to faint	*desmaiar*	dizhm*i*'ahr
fainting (-fit)	*desmaio* m.	dizhm*i*'oo
fatigued	*cansado, -a*	ku*n*(*g*)sah'doo, -e(r)
the fever	*a febre*	e(r) feb'ri
the fracture	*a fractura*	e(r) frahtoo're(r)
the gout	*a gota*	e(r) gaw'te(r)
headache	*dôr de cabeça*	dohr di ke(r)bes'se(r)
hoarse	*rouco, -a*	roh'koo, roh'ke(r)
the hospital	*o hospital*	oo ooshpitahl'
ill, sick	*doente ; enfermo, -a*	dooen'ti ; i*n*(*g*)fair'moo, [-e(r)
indigestion	*indigestão* f.	indi-zhishtow*n*(*g*)'
indisposed	*indisposto, -a*	indishpawsh'too, -e(r)
the indisposition	*a indisposição*	e(r) indishpoozisow*n*(*g*)'
inflammation	*inflammação* f.	i*n*(*g*)flummussow*n*(*g*)'
lame	*côxo, -a*	koh'shoo, -e(r)
the medicine	*a medicina*	e(r) midisee'ne(r)
the nurse	*a enfermeira*	e(r) i*n*(*g*)fermay're(r)

English.	Portuguese.	Pronunciation.
the ointment	*o unguento*	oo oo*n*(*g*)gwen'too
the pain	*a dôr*	e(r) dohr
paralysis	*paralysia* f.	purre(r)liz-ee'e(r)
a pill	*uma pilula*	oom'e(r) peel'oole(r)
the poison	*o veneno*	oo vin-en'oo [me(r)
a poultice (large)	*uma cataplasma*	oom'e(r) kutte(r)plahzh'-
— — (small)	*um sinapismo*	oo*n*(*g*) seene(r)peezh'moo
the prescription	*a receita*	e(r) ri-say'te(r)
the remedy	*o remedio*	oo ri-med'ioo
a rest	*um descanço*	oo*n*(*g*) dishku*n*(*g*)'soo
a scald	*uma escaldadura*	oom'e(r) ishkahlde(r)-doo're(r)
a scratch	*uma arranhadura*	oom' e(r) urrun-ye(r)doo'-
the sea-sickness	*o enjôo* [*ganta*	oo i*n*(*g*)zhoh'oo [re(r)
a sore throat	*dôres* (f.pl.) *de gar-*	doh'rizh di gurrgun'te(r)
a sprain	*uma torcedura*	oom'e(r) toorsidoo're(r)
the sting	*a picada*	e(r) peekah'de(r)
a tonic	*um tonico*	oo*n*(*g*) taw'nikoo
the wound	*a ferida*	e(r) ferree'de(r)

14. Food and Drink. *(A Comida e a Bebida.)*

(See also pages 14 to 19, and for Conversations see pages 102 to 105.)

English.	Portuguese.	Pronunciation.
Bacon	*toucinho* m.	tohseen'yoo
beef	*carne* (f.) *de vacca*	kahr'ni di vah'ke(r)
beef-steak	*bife* m.	beef'i
beer	*cerrêja* f.	serrvay'zhe(r)
a bottle	*uma garrafa*	oom'e(r) gurrah'fe(r)
the bread	*o pão*	oo pow*n*(*g*)
bread, brown	*pão* (m.) *de rala*	pow*n*(*g*) di rah'le(r)
—, new	— *fresco*	— fresh'koo
—, stale	— *duro*	— doo'roo
—, white	— *branco*	— bru*n*(*g*)'koo
the breakfast	*o almôço*	oo ahlmoh'soo
butter	*manteiga* f.	muntay'ghe(r)
a cake	*um bôlo*	oo*n*(*g*) boh'loo
calf's head	*cabeça de vitella*	kubbes'se(r) di veetel'le(r)
cheese	*queijo* m.	kay'zhoo
chocolate	*chocolate* m.	shookoolah'ti
a cigar	*um charuto*	oo*n*(*g*) shurroot'oo
claret	*vinho* (m.) *tinto*	veen'yoo teen'too

English.	Portuguese.	Pronunciation.
coffee	*café* m.	kuffay'
the cream	*a nata*	e(r) nah'te(r)
the dinner	*o jantar*	oo zhuntahr'
eggs	*ovos* m.pl.	aw'voozh
—, poached	— *escalfados*	— ishkahlfah'doozh
fat	*gordura* f.	goordoo're(r)
the flour	*a farinha*	e(r) furreen'ye(r)
ham	*prezunto* m.	prizoon'too
hock (wine)	*vinho de Hock*	veen'yoo di awk
the honey	*o mel*	oo mel
hunger	*fóme* f.	faw'mi
the ice, ice cream	*o gêlo, sorvêto*	oo zhel'oo, soorvet'i
jam	*dôce* f.	doh'si
kidney	*rim* m.	reen(*g*)
lamb	*cordeiro* m.	koorday'roo
the lean	*o magro*	oo mah'groo
lemonade	*limonada* f.	leemoonah'de(r)
meat	*carne* f.	kahr'ni
—, boiled	— *cosida*	— koozee'de(r)
—, roast	— *assada*	— ussah'de(r)
milk	*leite* m.	lay'ti
mustard	*mostarda* f.	mooshtahr'de(r)
mutton	*carne* (f.) *de carneiro*	kahr'ni di kurrnay'roo
oil	*azeite* m.	e(r)zay'ti
an olive	*uma azeitona*	oom'e(r) e(r)zaytoh'ne(r)
an omelet	*uma fritada d'ovos*	oom'e(r) freetah'de(r) daw'voozh
an onion	*uma cebola*	oom'e(r) siboh'ler
pepper	*pimenta* f.	peemen'te(r)
pork	*carne* (f.) *de porco*	kahr'ni di pohr'koo
port wine	*vinho* (m.) *do Porto*	veen'yoo doo pohr'too
a pudding	*um pudim*	oon(*g*) poodeen(*g*)'
rice	*arroz* m.	urrozh'
a roll	*um pãosinho*	oon(*g*) pown(*g*)zeen'yoo
salad	*salada* f.	se(r)lah'de(r)
salt	*sal* m.	sahl
a sausage	*uma salchicha*	oom'e(r) sahlshee'she(r)
sherry	*vinho* (m.) *de Xerez*	veen'yoo di sheh-raizh'
soda water	*agua* (f.) *de soda*	ah'gwe(r) di saw'de(r)
soup	*sôpa* f.	soh'pe(r)

English.	Portuguese.	Pronunciation.
sugar	*assucar* m.	ussoo'kurr
supper	*ceia* f.	say'e(r)
a syphon	*um syphão*	oo*n*(*g*) seefow*n*(*g*)'
tea	*chá* m.	shah
thirst	*sêde* f.	seh'di
tobacco	*tabaco* m.	te(r)bah'koo
under-done	*com sangue*	koo*n*(*g*) su*n*(*g*)'ghi
veal	*carne de vitella*	kahr'ni di veetel'le(r)
vegetables	*hortaliças* f.pl.	awrtullee'suzh
vinegar	*vinagre* m.	veenah'gri
water	*agua* f.	ah'gwe(r)
well-done	*bem cozido*	bai*n*(*g*) koozee'doo
wine	*vinho* m.	veen'yoo

15. Eating and Cooking Utensils.

(Utensilios de Mesa e de Cozinhar.)

(For Shopping, see p. 109.)

A basin	*um alguidar*	oo*n*(*g*) ahl-ghidahr'
a bowl	*uma tijella*	oom'e(r) teezhel'le(r)
the coffee-pot	*a cafeteira*	e(r) kuffitay're(r)
the cruet	*o galheteiro*	oo gul-yi-tay'roo
a cup	*uma chicara*	oom'e(r) shee'kurre(r)
the decanter	*a garrafa*	e(r) gurrah'fe(r)
the dish	*a travessa*	e(r) truvves'se(r)
the dish-cover	*o cobre-prato*	oo kaw'bri-prah'too
a fork	*um garfo*	oo*n*(*g*) gahr'foo
the frying-pan	*a sartã, frigideira*	e(r) surrtu*n*(*g*),' frizhiday're(r)
a glass (tumbler)	*um copo*	oo*n*(*g*) kaw'poo
a gridiron	*uma grelha*	oom'e(r) grel'ye(r)
the kettle	*a chaleira*	e(r) she(r)lay're(r)
a knife	*uma faca*	oom'e(r) fah'ke(r)
a lid	*uma tampa*	oom'e(r) tum'pe(r)
the nut-crackers	*o quebranozes*	oo kaibre(r)naw'zizh
the oven	*o fôrno*	oo fohr'noo
a pan	*uma cassarola*	oom'e(r) kusseraw'le(r)
a plate	*um prato*	oo*n*(*g*) prah'too
a saucepan, pot	*uma panella*	oom'e(r) pun-el'le(r)
a saucer	*um pires*	oo*n*(*g*) pee'rizh
a serviette	*um guardanapo*	oo*n*(*g*) gwurrdun-ah'poo

English.	Portuguese.	Pronunciation.
the soup ladle	*a colher da sôpa*	e(r) kool-yair' de(r) soh'-
a spoon	*uma colher*	oom'e(r) kool-yair' [pe(r)
the stove	*a fogão*	oo foogown(g)' [ze(r)
the table-cloth	*a toalha de mesa*	e(r) too-i'l-ye(r) di mai'-
table-spoon	*colher* (f.) *de mesa*	kool-yair' di mai'ze(r)
the tea-pot	*o bulle*	oo bool'li [shah
a tea-spoon	*uma colher de chá*	oom'e(r) kool-yair' di
the tray	*a bandeja*	e(r) bundai'zhe(r)
a wineglass	*um calix*	oon(g) kah'leezh

16. Dress and Dressing. *(O Vestuario.)*

(See also Vocab. 17, and Shopping, Dressmaker, Shoemaker, Laundress, pp. 109 to 113.)

The blouse	*a blusa*	e(r) bloo'ze(r)
the boot-jack	*o descalçador*	oo dishkahlse(r)dohr'
the bracelet	*a pulseira*	e(r) poolsay're(r)
the braces	*os suspensorios*	oozh sooshpensaw'ri-
the brooch	*o broche*	oo braw'shi [oozh
the brush	*a escova*	e(r) iskoh've(r)
the buttons	*os botões*	oozh bootoy'n(g)zh
the button-hook	*o abotoador*	oo e(r)bootoo-e(r)dohr'
the calico	*o morim*	oo mooreen(g)'
the cap	*o bonet*	oo boh'nay
a cloak, cape	*uma capa*	oom'e(r) kah'pe(r)
the cloth	*o panno*	oo pun'noo [too
the clothes-brush	*a escova de fato*	e(r) ishkoh've(r) di fah'-
a coat	*um casaco*	oon(g) ke(r)zah'koo
a coat (great-)	*um casacão*	oon(g) kuzze(r)kown(g)'
the comb	*o pente*	oo pen'ti
the cotton	*o algodão*	oo ahlgoodow(n)g'
the cravat	*a gravata* [m.	e(r) gruvvah'te(r)
dress (clothing)	*fato* m., *vestimento*	fah'too, vishtimen'too
dress-clothes	*traje* (m.) *de etiquet-*	trah'zhi di itiket'te(r)
a dressing-gown	*um roupão* [*ta*	oon(g) rohpown(g)'
the flannel	*a flanella*	e(r) flun-el'le(r)
the flannelette	*a bactilha*	e(r) bayteel'ye(r)
the gaiters, leg-	*as polainas*	uzh pooli'nuzh
the garters [gings	*as ligas*	uzh lee'guzh
the gloves	*as luvas*	uzh loo'vuzh
the hair-pin	*o gancho de cabello*	oo gun(g)'shoo di ke(r)-
the hat	*o chapeu*	oo she(r)peh'oo [bel'loo

English.	Portuguese.	Pronunciation.
the hat (opera-)	*o chapeu de molas*	oo she(r)peh'oo di maw'-
a hole	*um buraco*	oo*n*(*g*) boorah'koo [luzh
the hood	*o capuz*	oo ke(r)poozh'
jewellery	*joias* f.pl.	zhoy'uzh
the lace	*a renda*	e(r) ren'de(r)
the linen	*a roupa branca*	e(r) roh'pe(r) bru*n*(*g*)'-
the lining	*o fôrro*	oo fohr'roo [ke(r)
a mackintosh, *or*	*um sobretudo imper-*	oo*n*(*g*) sohbritoo'doo
waterproof coat	*meavel*	ee*n*(*g*)perrmiah'vel
the muslin	*a cassa*	e(r) kahs'se(r)
the nail-brush	*a escova de unhas*	e(r) ishkoh've(r) di oon'-
a necklace	*um collar*	oo*n*(*g*) koollahr' [yuzh
a necktie	*uma gravata*	oom'e(r) gruvvah'te(r)
a needle	*uma agulha*	oom'e(r) e(r)gool'ye(r)
an overcoat	*um sobretudo*	oo*n*(*g*) sohbritoo'doo
the parasol	*a sombrinha*	e(r) sohmbreen'ye(r)
the pins	*os alfinetes*	ooz ahlfin-et'izh
the pocket	*a algibeira*	e(r) ahl-zhibay're(r)
the purse	*a bolsa*	e(r) bohl'se(r) [be(r)
razor	*navalha* (f.) *de barba*	ne(r)v*i*'l-ye(r) di bahr'-
a ring	*um annel*	oo*n*(*g*) unnel' [de(r)
the safety-pin	*o alfinete de fralda*	oo ahlfinet'i di frahl'-
sewing-cotton	*algodão* (m.) *de*	ahlgoodow*n*(*g*)' di koo-
sewing-silk	*retroz* m. [*coser*	ritrawzh' [sehr'
the shirt-front	*o peitilho da camisa*	oo payteel'yoo de(r)
		ke(r)mee'ze(r)
the shoe-horn	*a calçadeira*	e(r) kahlse(r)day're(r)
the silk	*a sêda*	e(r) seh'de(r)
the skirt	*a saia*	e(r) s*i*'e(r)
soap	*sabão* m.	se(r)bow*n*(*g*)'
a stud	*um botão*	oo*n*(*g*) bootow*n*(*g*)'
suit of clothes	*vestimento* (m.) *com-*	vishtimen'too koomplai'-
the thread	*a linha* [*pleto*	e(r) leen'ye(r) [too
the tooth-brush	*a escova de dentes*	e(r) ishkoh've(r) di den'-
the trousers	*as calças*	uzh kahl'suzh [tizh
the umbrella	*o guardachuva*	oo gwahrde(r)shoo've(r)
the veil	*o véo*	oo veh'oo
the walking-stick,	*a bengala*	e(r) bengah'le(r)
a watch [cane	*um relogio*	oo*n*(*g*) rilaw'zhioo
the wool	*a lã*	e(r) lu*n*(*g*)

17. Washing Lists.* (*Roes da Roupa suja.*)

FOR LADIES. (*Para Senhoras.*)

(For Conversations, see pp. 112-3.)

English.	Portuguese.	Pronunciation.
Apron, pinafore	*avental* m.	e(r)ventahl'
Bodice	*corpinho* m.	koorpeen'yoo
Cap	*touca* f.	toh'ke(r)
Chemise	*camisa* f.	ke(r)meez'e(r)
Drawers	*calças* f.pl.	kahl'suzh
Dress	*vestido* m.	vishtee'doo
Dressing-gown	*roupão* m. [*tarios*	rohpown(g)' [oozh
Napkins	*pannos* (m.pl.) *sani-*	pun'noozh sunnitah'ri-
Night-caps	*toucas de dormir*	toh'kuzh di doo'r-meer
Night-gowns	*camisas de dormir*	ke(r)mee'zuzh di doo'r-
Petticoat	*saiote* m.	si-aw'ti [meer
—, flannel	*saiote de flanella*	si-aw'ti di flun-el'le(r)
Serviettes	*guardanapos* m.pl.	gwahrde(r)nah'poozh
Silk stockings	*meias* (f.pl.) *de sêda*	may'uzh di seh'de(r)
Sleeves	*mangas* f.pl.	mun(g)'guzh
Stays	*espartilhos* m.pl.	ishpurteel'yoozh
Towels	*toalhas* f.pl.	too-i'l-yuzh

FOR GENTLEMEN. (*Para Homens*)

English.	Portuguese.	Pronunciation.
Collars	*collarinhos* m.pl.	koollurreen'yoozh
Cuffs	*punhos* m.pl.	poon'yoozh
Flannel waistcoat	*collete de flanella*	kollet'i di flun-el'le(r)
Neckties	*gravatas* f.pl.	gruv-aht'uzh
Night-shirts	*camisas de dormir*	ke(r)mee'zuzh di doo'r-
Pants (drawers)	*ceroulas* f.pl.	siroh'luzh [meer
Pocket handker-	*lenços* m.pl.	len'soozh
Shirts [chiefs	*camisas* f.pl.	ke(r)mee'zuzh
Silk handkerchiefs	*lenços de sêda*	len'soozh di seh'de(r)
Socks	*piugas* f.pl.	peeoo'guzh
Stockings	*meias* f.pl.	may'uzh
Trousers	*calças* f.pl.	kahl'suzh
Under-vest	*camisola* f.	kummizaw'le(r)
Waistcoat (vest)	*collete* m.	kollet'i

* THIMM (C. A.) **Portuguese Washing Book for Ladies and Gentlemen. With Counterfoils in English, alphabetically arranged for practical use by Tourists and others.** Red wrapper, 8vo. **6d.**

18. House and Furniture. *(Casa e Mobilia.)*

(See also Vocabulary 15, p. 30, and Shopping, p. 100.)

English.	Portuguese.	Pronunciation.
The ante-room	*a antesala*	e(r) unti-sah'le(r)
an armchair	*uma cadeira de braços*	oom'e(r) ke(r)day're(r) di brah'soozh
the ashes	*as cinzas*	uzh seen(*g*)'zuzh
the balcony	*a varanda*	e(r) vurrun'de(r)
a basket	*um cêsto*	oon(*g*) sesh'too
the bed	*a cama*	e(r) kum'e(r)
the bedroom	*o quarto de cama*	oo kwahr'too di kum'e(r)
a bedstead	*um leito*	oon(*g*) lay'too
a blanket	*um cobertor*	oon(*g*) kooberrtohr'
the blind	*a persiana*	e(r) perrsi-un'e(r)
the book-shelf	*a estante dos livros*	e(r) ishtun'ti doozh leev'roozh
a box	*uma caixa*	oom'e(r) ki'she(r)
the broom	*a vassoura*	e(r) vussoh're(r)
the candle	*a vella*	e(r) vel'le(r)
the candlestick	*o castiçal*	oo ke(r)shti-sahl'
the carpet	*o tapête*	oo te(r)pet'i
the ceiling	*o tecto*	oo teh'too
the cellar	*o sotão*	oo sootown(*g*)'
a chair	*uma cadeira*	oom'e(r) ke(r)day're(r)
the chamber utensil	*o ourinol*	oo ohreenawl'
the chest of drawers	*a commoda*	e(r) kawm'moo-de(r)
the chimney	*a chaminé*	e(r) shum-eenay'
a clock	*um relogio*	oon(*g*) rilaw'zhioo
the closet (w.c.)	*a latrina*	e(r) le(r)tree'ne(r)
coal	*carvão* m.	kurrvown(*g*)'
the corridor	*o corredor*	oo koorridohr'
the couch	*o sofá*	oo soofah'
the counterpane	*a colcha*	e(r) kawl'she(r)
the courtyard	*o pateo*	oo pah'tioo
a cupboard	*um armario*	oon(*g*) ahrmah'rioo
the curtain	*o cortinado*	oo koortinah'doo
a cushion	*uma almofada*	oom'e(r) ahlmoofah'de(r)
the dining-room	*a sala de jantar*	e(r) sah'le(r) di zhuntahr'
the door	*a porta*	e(r) pawr'te(r)
the door-bell	*a campaínha*	e(r) kumpe(r)een'ye(r)

English.	Portuguese.	Pronunciation.
the drawing-room	*a sala de visitas*	e(r) sah'le(r) di vizee'-tuzh
an easy-chair	*uma cadeira de regalo*	oom'e(r) ke(r)day're(r) di rigah'loo
the electric light	*a luz electrica*	e(r) loozh ilay'trike(r)
the fender	*a defensa do fogão*	e(r) difen(g)'se(r) doo foo-gown(g)'
the fire-place	*o fogão*	oo foo-gown(g)'
the flame	*a chamma*	e(r) shum'me(r)
the floor	*o sobrado*	oo soobrah'doo
— — (first)	*o primeiro andar*	oo preemay'roo undahr'
— — (ground)	*o rez do chão*	oo ray doo shown(g)
a footstool	*um banquinho para os pés*	oon(g) bun(g)keen'yoo pur're(r) oozh paizh
the garden	*o jardim*	oo zhurrdeen(g)'
the key	*a chave*	e(r) shah'vi
the kitchen	*a cozinha*	e(r) koozeen'ye(r)
the kitchen dresser	*o aparador da cozinha*	oo up-urre(r)dohr' de(r) koozeen'ye(r)
the lamp	*o candieiro*	oo kundiay'roo
the landing	*o patamar*	oo pe(r)te(r)mahr'
the larder	*a despensa*	e(r) dishpen(g)'se(r)
the library	*a bibliotheca*	e(r) beebliootay'ke(r)
the light, candle	*a luz, vella*	e(r) loozh, vel'le(r)
the lock	*a fechadura*	e(r) fishe(r)doo're(r)
a looking-glass	*um espelho*	oon(g) ishpel'yoo
the matches	*os phosphoros*	oozh fawsh'fooroozh
the mattress	*o colchão*	oo kawlshown(g)'
the night commode	*a cadeira de noite*	e(r) ke(r)day're(r) di noy'ti
the piano	*o piano*	oo pee-un'oo
a pillow	*uma almofada, travesseira*	oom'e(r) ahlmoofah'de(r), tre(r)vessay're(r)
the poker	*o atiçador*	oo e(r)tee-se(r)dohr'
the roof	*o telhado*	oo tilyah'doo
the room	*o quarto*	oo kwahr'too
a seat	*um assento*	oon(g) us-sen'too
the sheets	*os lençoes*	oozh len(g)soyzh'
the shovel	*a pá*	e(r) pah
the sideboard	*o aparador*	oo up-urre(r)dohr'
the smoke	*o fumo*	oo foo'moo
the soap	*o sabão*	oo se(r)bown(g)'

English.	Portuguese.	Pronunciation.
the soot	*a fuligem*	e(r) foolee'zhen(*g*)
a spark	*uma faisca*	oom'e(r) fe(r)eesh'ke(r)
the staircase	*a escada*	e(r) ishkah'de(r)
the stairs	*os degraos da escada*	oozh digrowzh' de(r) ish-kah'de(r)
a table	*uma mesa*	oom'e(r) mai'ze(r)
a table-cloth	*uma toalha (de mesa)*	oom'e(r) too-*i*'l-ye(r) [di mai'ze(r)]
the tiles	*as telhas*	uzh tel'yuzh
the tongs	*a tenaz*	e(r) tinazh'
a towel	*uma toalha*	oom'e(r) too-*i*'l-ye(r)
the wall	*a parêde*	e(r) purrai'di
a wax candle	*uma vella de cêra*	oom'e(r) vel'le(r) di sai'-re(r)
a vase	*um vaso*	oon(*g*) vah'zoo
the window	*a janella*	e(r) zhunnel'le(r)

19. Religion. *(Religião.)*

(See also Vocabulary 9, p. 22.)

English.	Portuguese.	Pronunciation.
Absolution	*absolução* f.	ahbsooloosown(*g*)'
the aisle	*a nave lateral*	e(r) nah'vi lutturahl'
the altar	*o altar*	oo ahltahr'
the baptism	*o baptismo*	oo bahteezh'moo
Bible Society	*a Sociedade Biblica*	e(r) soosi-e(r)dah'di beeb'lik-e(r)
the burial	*o enterro*	oo intair'roo
the cemetery	*o cemiterio*	oo simitair'ioo
the chancel	*o côro*	oo kaw'roo
the chapel	*a capella*	e(r) ke(r)pel'le(r)
the choir	*os coristas*	oozh kooreesh'tuzh
the church	*a igreja*	e(r) eegray'zhe(r)
the clergyman	*o clerigo*	oo klair'igoo
Communion	*communhão* f.	koommoon-yown(*g*)'
a fast-day	*um dia de jejum*	oon(*g*) dee'e(r) di zhi-zhoo(*n*)*g*'
a festival	*uma festa*	oom'e(r) fesh'te(r)
the font	*a pia baptismal*	e(r) pee'e(r) bahteezh-mahl'
a grave	*uma sepultura*	oom'e(r) sipooltoo're(r)
a hymn-book	*um livro de hymnos*	oon(*g*) leev'roo di ee'-noozh
the lectern	*a estante*	e(r) ishtun'ti
the litany	*a ladaínha*	e(r) lud-e(r)een'ye(r)

English.	Portuguese.	Pronunciation.
mass, high	*missa* (f.) *cantada*	mees'se(r) kuntah'de(r)
—, low	— *rezada*	— rizah'de(r)
matins	*matinas* f.pl.	me(r)tee'nuzh
the nave	*a nave*	e(r) nah'vi
the offertory	*o offertorio*	oo ohffurrtaw'rioo
the organ	*o orgão*	oo awr'gown(g)
the organist	*o organista*	oo awrgun-eesh'te(r)
the penance	*a penitencia*	e(r) peniten'si-e(r)
a prayer	*uma oração*	oom'e(r) awre(r)sown(g)'
— — -book	*um livro de orações*	oon(g) lee'vroo di awre(r)soy'n(g)zh
the priest	*o padre*	oo pah'dri
a Protestant	*um Protestante*	oon(g) prootishtun'ti
the pulpit	*o pulpito*	oo pool'pitoo
a Roman Catholic	*um Catholico Romano*	oon(g) ke(r)tawl'ikoo roomun'oo
the sacrament	*o sacramento*	oo se(r)kre(r)men'too
sacred	*sagrad-o, -a*	se(r)grah'd-oo, -e(r)
salvation	*salvação* f.	sahlve(r)sown(g)'
service, divine	*serviço* (m.) *divino*	serrvee'soo divee'noo
—, the morning	*a reza da manhã*	e(r) rai'ze(r) de(r) mun[yun(g)'
—, the evening	— — — *tarde*	— — — tahr'di
the verger	*o sacristão*	oo se(r)krishtown(g)'
vespers	*vesperas* f.pl.	vesh'peruzh

20. Legal and Judicial Terms.

(Termos Legaes e Juridicos.)

English.	Portuguese.	Pronunciation.
Acquittal	*absolvição* f.	ahbsawlvisown(g)'
an action	*um processo*	oon(g) prooses'soo
advance money, to	*adiantar dinheiro*	e(r)diuntahr' din-yair'oo
affidavit	*declaracão* f., *ajuramentada*	diklurre(r)sown(g)' e(r)-zhoore(r)-mentah'de(r)
the agreement	*o convenio*	oo kohnven'ioo
the allegation	*a allegação*	e(r) ul-leg-ussown(g)'
allege, to	*allegar*	ul-leg-ahr'
an apology	*uma apologia*	oom'e(r) e(r)pohloh-[zhee'e(r)
arbitrate, to	*arbitrar*	ahrbitrahr'
arbitration	*arbitramento* m.	ahrbitre(r)men'too
the arrangement	*o accôrdo*	oo uk-kohr'doo

English.	Portuguese.	Pronunciation.
the arrears	*os atrazos*	ooz ut-rah'zoozh
arrest, to	*prender*	prendehr'
attest, to	*attestar*	ut-teshtahr'
the attestation	*o attestado*	oo ut-teshtah'doo
the attorney	*o procurador*	oo prookoore(r)dohr'
attorney, power of	*procuração* f.	prookoor-ussow*n*(*g*)'
authorise, to	*autorizar*	owtoorizahr'
the award	*o arbitrio*	oo ahrbee'trioo
the bail	*a fiança*	e(r) feeu*n*(*g*)'se(r)
the bailiff	*o meirinho*	oo may-reen'yoo
bond (for loan)	*uma obrigação*	oom'e(r) awbree-gus-[sow*n*(*g*)'
the case	*a causa*	e(r) kow'ze(r)
— — for the prosecution [fence	*o processo accusatorio*	oo prooses'soo e(r)koo-ze(r)taw'rioo
— — for the de-	— — *defensorio*	— — difensaw'rioo
the charge (accusa-[tion)	*a accusação*	e(r) ukkoozussow*n*(*g*)'
charge, to	*accusar*	ukkoozahr'
the claimant	*o pretendente*	oo pritenden'ti
a client	*um cliente*	oo*n*(*g*) kli-en'ti
the complainant	*o autor*	oo owtohr'
the conviction	*a convicção*	e(r) koh*n*(*g*)veeksow*n*(*g*)'
a court of justice	*um tribunal de justiça*	oo*n*(*g*) treeboonahl' di zhooshtee'se(r)
criminal, *adj.*	*criminal*	kreemeenahl'
decision (of a case)	*decisão* f.	dissizow*n*(*g*)'
the deed of sale	*a escritura de venda*	e(r) ishkreetoo're(r) di [vend'e(r)
— — of assignment	— — *de transferencia*	— — di tru*n*(*g*)sh-ferren'si-e(r)
the defence	*a defesa*	e(r) difez'ze(r)
defend, to (in court)	*defender*	difendehr'
the defendant	*o réo*	oo reh'oo
the deposition	*o depoimento*	oo dipoymen'too
the effects (goods)	*os effeitos*	ooz iffay'toozh
the embezzlement	*a peculação*	e(r) pikool-ussow*n*(*g*)'
equity	*direito* m.	diray'too
the estate	*a propriedade*	e(r) prohpri-e(r)dah'di
estate, real and personal	*bens de raiz e moveis*	bai*n*(*g*)zh di re(r)eezh' ee maw'vezh
the evidence	*as provas*	uzh praw'vuzh
the excise	*a siza*	e(r) see'ze(r)

English.	Portuguese.	Pronunciation.
the executor	*o testamenteiro*	oo tishte(r)mentay'roo
the fee (of office)	*o emolumento*	oo imooloomen'too
a fine (payment in money)	*uma mulcta*	oom'e(r) mool'te(r)
a forgery	*uma falsificação*	oom'e(r) fahlsifeekus-sown(g)'
a fraud	*uma fraude*	oom'e(r) frow'di
fraudulent	*fraudulento, -a*	frowdoolen'too, -e(r)
illegal	*illegal*	illigahl'
imprisonment	*encarceramento* m.	in(g)kahrserre(r)men'too
an information	*uma informação*	oom'e(r) een(g)foormus-sown(g)'
an injunction	*uma prohibição*	oom'e(r) proo-eebi-sown(g)'
the injustice	*a injustiça*	e(r) een(g)zhooshtee'se(r)
an inventory	*um inventario*	oon(g) een(g)ventah'rioo
the jail	*a cadeia*	e(r) ke(r)day'e(r)
the judge	*o juiz*	oo zhoo-eezh'
judgment, to give	*passar sentença*	pus-sahr' senten(g)'se(r)
jurisdiction	*jurisdicção* f.	zhooreezhdee'sown(g)
the jury	*o jury*	oo zhoo'ri
a justice of the peace	*um juiz de paz*	oon(g) zhoo-eezh' di pahzh
law, the civil	*a lei civil*	e(r) lay seeveel'
—, — criminal	*— — criminal*	— — kreemeenahl'
a law-suit	*uma demanda*	oom'e(r) dimun'de(r)
a lawyer	*um advogado*	oon(g) udvoogah'doo
the lender	*o emprestador*	oo impreshte(r)dohr'
non-suit, to	*sentenciar á revelia*	senten(g)siahr' ah revel-ee'e(r)
an oath	*um juramento*	oon(g) zhoore(r)men'too
— —, to take	*prestar juramento*	prishtahr' zhoore(r)men'too
the parties (in suit)	*as partes*	uzh pahr'tizh
penal	*penal*	pinahl'
perjury	*perjurio* m.	purrzhoo'rioo
the petitioner	*o supplicante*	oo sooplikun'ti
the plaintiff	*o pleiteante*	oo playti-un'ti
the police	*a policia*	e(r) poolee'si-e(r)
— — office	*a repartição da policia*	e(r) ripurrtissown(g)' de(r) poolee'sie(r)
the procedure (legal)	*o procedimento legal*	oo proo-sidimen'too ligahl'
the proof	*a prova*	e(r) praw've(r)
the prosecution	*a perseguição*	e(r) perrsi-ghissown(g)'

English.	Portuguese.	Pronunciation.
the prosecutor	*o accusador*	oo e(r)kooze(r)dohr'
the punishment	*o castigo*	oo kushtee'goo
the release	*a soltura*	e(r) sawltoo're(r)
the robbery	*o roubo*	oo roh'boo
the seal	*o sêllo*	oo sel'loo
seal, to	*sellar*	sellahr'
the sentence	*a sentença*	e(r) senten(g)'se(r)
the statement	*a declaração*	e(r) diklurre(r)sown(g)'
the statute	*o estatuto*	oo ishte(r)too'too
sue, to	*demandar*	dimundahr'
the suit	*o pleito*	oo play'too
a summons	*uma citação*	oom'e(r) seetussown(g)'
the surety [house)	*o fiançador*	oo fi-un(g)'se(r)dohr
the tenant (of a	*o inquilino*	oo in(g)kilee'noo
the testament (will)	*o testamento*	oo tishte(r)m-en'too
the testator	*o testador*	oo tishte(r)dohr'
the theft	*o furto*	oo foor'too
the thief	*o ladrão*	oo le(r)drown(g)'
the trial	*o julgamento*	oo zhoolge(r)men'too
trial by jury	— — *por jury*	— — poor zhoo'ri
unlawful	*illegal*	illigahl'
valid	*valido*	vah'lidoo
the witness	*a testemunha*	e(r) tishtimoon'ye(r)
a writ	*uma citação*	oom'e(r) seetussown(g)'

21. Professions and Trades. (*Profissões e Officios.*)

(For Shopping, see p. 109.)

English.	Portuguese.	Pronunciation.
An actor	*um actor*	oon(g) ahtohr'
an actress	*uma actriz*	oom'e(r) ahtreezh'
an architect	*um architecto*	oon(g) ahrkitet'oo
an artisan	*um operario*	oon(g) ahrteesh'te(r)
an artist	*um artista*	oon(g) awperahr'ioo
a baker	*um padeiro*	oon(g) pahday'roo
a banker	*um banqueiro*	oon(g) bunkay'roo
a bookseller	*um livreiro*	oon(g) leevray'roo
a brewer	*um cervejeiro*	oon(g) surrvi-zhay'roo
a butcher	*um carniceiro*	oon(g) kurrneesay'roo
a carpenter	*um carpinteiro*	oon(g) kurrpintay'roo
a chemist	*um pharmaceutico*	oon(g) furrmusseh'ooti-
a clergyman	*um clerigo*	oon(g) klair'igoo [koo

English.	Portuguese.	Pronunciation.
a clerk	*um caixeiro*	oo*n*(*g*) k*i*-shay'roo
a coachman	*um cocheiro*	oo*n*(*g*) kooshay'roo
a commercial traveller	*um viajante commercial*	oo*n*(*g*) vee-e(r)zhun'ti koomerrseeahl'
a confectioner	*um confeiteiro*	oo*n*(*g*) kohnfaytay'roo
a consul	*um consul*	oo*n*(*g*) kohn'sool
cook	*cozinheiro* m., *-a* f.	koozin-yay'roo, -e(r)
a cycle-maker	*um fabricante de velocipedes*	oo*n*(*g*) fub-reekahn'ti di' vilawsiped'izh
a dentist	*um dentista*	oo*n*(*g*) denteesh'te(r)
a doctor	*um doutor*	oo*n*(*g*) dohtohr'
an engineer	*um engenheiro*	oo*n*(*g*) i*n*(*g*)zhin-yay'roo
a farmer	*um lavrador*	oo*n*(*g*) luvre(r)dohr'
a farrier	*um ferrador*	oo*n*(*g*) ferre(r)dohr'
a fencing-master	*um mestre de esgrima*	oo*n*(*g*) mesh'tri di izh-gree'me(r)
a fisherman	*um pescador*	oo*n*(*g*) pishke(r)dohr'
a florist	*um florista*	oo*n*(*g*) floo-reesh'te(r)
a goldsmith	*um ourives*	oo*n*(*g*) ohree'vizh
a governess	*uma mestra*	oom'e(r) mesh'tre(r)
a grocer	*um especieiro*	oo*n*(*g*) ishpissiay'roo
a hairdresser	*um cabelleireiro*	oo*n*(*g*) ke(r)bellay'rayroo
a hatter	*um chapelleiro*	oo*n*(*g*) she(r)pellay'roo
a jeweller	*um joalheiro*	oo*n*(*g*) zhoo-ul-yay'roo
the laundress	*a lavadeira*	e(r) luvve(r)day're(r)
a merchant	*um negociante*	oo*n*(*g*) nigoosiun'ti
a miller	*um moleiro*	oo*n*(*g*) moolay'roo
a milliner	*uma modista de chapeos*	oom'e(r) moodeesh'te(r) di she(r)peh'oozh
a money-changer	*um cambista*	oo*n*(*g*) kum-beesh'te(r)
a nurse (hospital)	*uma enfermeira*	oome(r)i*n*(*g*)ferrmay're(r)
an optician	*um oculista*	oo*n*(*g*) awkooleesh'te(r)
a painter	*um pintor*	oo*n*(*g*) peentohr'
a photographer	*um photographo*	oo*n*(*g*) foo-tawg'ruf-oo
a policeman	*um policia*	oo*n*(*g*) poolee'si-e(r)
a porter (commissionaire)	*um môço de fretes*	oo*n*(*g*) moh'soo di fret'izh
the postmaster	*o administrador do correio*	oo udminishtre(r)dohr' doo koorray'oo
a printer	*um typographo*	oo*n*(*g*) tipaw'gre(r)foo
a professor	*um professor*	oo*n*(*g*) proofessohr'

English.	Portuguese.	Pronunciation.
a saddler	*um selleiro*	oo*n*(*g*) sellay'roo
schoolmaster	*mestre* (m.) *de escola*	mesh'tri di ishkaw'le(r)
servant	*criado* m., *criada* f.	kreeah'doo, kreeah'de(r)
a shoemaker	*um sapateiro*	oo*n*(*g*) suppe(r)tay'roo
a shopkeeper	*um logista*	oo*n*(*g*) loozheesh'te(r)
a singer	*um cantor* m., *uma cantora* f.	oo*n*(*g*) kuntohr', oom'e(r) kuntaw're(r)
a smith	*um serralheiro, ferreiro*	oo*n*(*g*) serrulyay'roo, ferray'roo
a soldier	*um soldado*	oo*n*(*g*) sawldah'doo
a student	*um estudante*	oo*n*(*g*) ishtoodun'ti
a surgeon	*um cirurgião*	oo*n*(*g*) si-roorzhiow*n*(*g*)'
a surveyor	*um medidor de terrenos*	oo*n*(*g*) middeedohr' di terren'oozh
a tailor	*um alfayate*	oo*n*(*g*) ahlfayah'ti
teacher	*preceptor* m., *—a* f.	preeseptohr',preeseptawr-e(r)
a watchmaker	*um relojoeiro*	oo*n*(*g*) riloozhooay'roo

22. Ships and Shipping. *(Navios e Navegação.)*

(For Steamboat, see page 97.)

The anchor	*a ancora*	e(r) u*n*(*g*)'koore(r)
the berth	*o beliche*	oo bilee'shi
the boat	*o bote*	oo baw'ti
the bow	*a prôa*	e(r) proh'e(r)
the cabin	*a camara*	e(r) kum'urre(r)
the cable	*a amarra*	e(r) um-ahr're(r)
the captain	*o capitão*	oo ke(r)pitow*n*(*g*)'
the compass	*a bitacola*	e(r) beetah'koole(r)
the course	*o rumo*	oo roo'moo
the crew	*a tripulação*	e(r) treepoolussow*n*(*g*)'
the deck	*o convez*	oo koh*n*(*g*)vezh'
the ebb	*a vasante*	e(r) vuzzun'ti
the flag	*a bandeira*	e(r) bunday're(r)
the flow	*a enchente*	e(r) i*n*(*g*)shen'ti
the harbour	*o porto de abrigo*	oo pohr'too di e(r)bree'-goo
the helm (rudder)	*o leme*	oo lem'i
the keel	*a quilha*	e(r) keel'ye(r)
the landing-stage	*o desembarcadouro*	oo dizimburrke(r)doh'roo
the life-buoy	*a boia de salvavidas*	e(r) boy'e(r) di salve(r)-vee'duzh
the light-house	*o pharol*	oo furrawl'

English.	Portuguese.	Pronunciation.
the mast	*o mastro*	oo mahsh'troo
the merchantman	*o navio mercante*	oo ne(r)vee'oo merr-
an oar	*um remo*	oo*n*(*g*) rem'oo [kun'ti
the pilot	*o practico, piloto*	oo prah'tikoo, peeloh'too
a pilot-boat	*um bote de practicos*	oo*n*(*g*) baw'ti di prah'-
the port	*o porto*	oo pohr'too [tikoozh
the porthole	*a portinhola*	e(r) poortin-yaw'le(r)
a rope	*um cabo*	oo*n*(*g*) kah'boo
the sail	*a vela*	e(r) vel'e(r)
the seaman (sailor)	*o marinheiro*	oo murrin-yay'roo
the sea-sickness	*o enjôo*	oo i*n*(*g*)zhoh'oo
the ship	*o navio*	oo ne(r)vee'oo
the steamboat	*o vapor*	oo ve(r)pohr' [re(r)
the steerage	*a terceira camara*	e(r) terrsay're(r) kum'ur-
the steersman	*o timoneiro*	oo teemoonay'roo
the stern	*a pôpa*	e(r) poh'pe(r)
the steward	*o despenseiro*	oo dishpensay'roo
the tug	*o rebocador*	oo ribooke(r)dohr'
the wharf	*o caes trapiche*	oo ki'zh tre(r)pee'shi

23. Travelling. *(Viajar.)*

(For Conversations see pages 96 to 99.)

The arrival	*a chegada*	e(r) shigah'de(r)
the bill	*a conta*	e(r) kohn'te(r)
the box	*a caixa*	e(r) ki'she(r)
the bridle	*o freio*	oo fray'oo
a cabman	*um cocheiro*	oo*n*(*g*) kooshay'roo
a carriage	*uma carruagem*	oom'e(r) kurrooi'zhe*n*(*g*)
the coach	*o coche*	oo kaw'shi
the coachman	*o cocheiro*	oo kooshay'roo
a cushion	*uma almofada*	oom'e(r) ahlmoofah'de(r)
the custom-house	*a alfandega*	e(r) ahlfun'di-ghe(r)
a custom-house officer	*um official da alfandega*	oo*n*(*g*) awfissiahl' de(r) ahlfun'di-ghe(r)
the departure	*a partida*	e(r) purrtee'de(r)
the engine	*a machina*	e(r) mah'keene(r)
the fare	*o preço do bilhete*	oo press'oo doo beel-yet'i
a foot-warmer	*um aquecedor de pés*	oo*n*(*g*) e(r)kess'idohr di
the guard	*o guarda*	oo gwahr'de(r) [paizh
a guide	*um guia*	oo*n*(*g*) ghee'e(r)

English.	Portuguese.	Pronunciation.
a guide-book	*um livro de guia*	oo*n*(*g*) lee'vroo di ghee'e(r)
a hat-box	*uma chapeleira*	oom'e(r) she(r)pel-ay're(r)
the hotel	*o hotel*	oo aw'tel
the interpreter	*o interprete*	oo eentair'pri-ti
the key	*a chave*	e(r) shah'vi
the landlady	*a patrôa*	e(r) pe(r)troh'e(r)
the landlord (of a hotel)	*o proprietario de um hotel*	oo proopri-eh-tah'rioo di oo*n*(*g*) aw'tel
the lavatory	*o lavadouro*	oo luvve(r)doh'roo
the luggage	*a bagagem*	e(r) be(r)gh*i*'zhe*n*(*g*)
the office	*o escriptorio*	oo ishkreetaw'rioo
an omnibus	*um omnibus*	oo*n*(*g*) aw'niboozh
the payment	*o pagamento*	oo pug-e(r)-men'too
the pier	*a ponte de desembarque*	e(r) pohn'ti di diz-im-bahr'ki
the porter	*o porteiro*	oo poortay'roo
the railway	*o caminho de ferro*	oo ke(r)meen'yoo di fair'-roo
the railway carriage	*a carruagem do caminho de ferro*	e(r) kurroo*i*'zhe*n*(*g*) doo ke(r)meen'yoo di fair'roo
the railway-station	*a estação do caminho de ferro*	e(r) ishtussow*n*(*g*)' doo ke(r)meen'yoo di fair'roo
a receipt	*um recibo*	oo*n*(*g*) risee'boo
the reins	*as redeas*	uzh rai'di-uzh
the road	*a estrada*	e(r) ishtrah'de(r)
a saddle	*uma sella*	oom'e(r) sel'le(r)
the saloon (aft)	*a primeira camara*	e(r) preemay're(r) kum'-urre(r)
the station-master	*o chefe da estação*	oo shef'i de(r) ishtus-sow*n*(*g*)'
the steamer	*o vapor*	oo ve(r)pohr'
a strap	*uma corrêa*	oom'e(r) koorray'e(r)
the ticket	*o bilhete de ida*	oo beel-yet'i di ee'de(r)
— —, return	*— — de volta*	— — di vawl'te(r)
the ticket-office	*a bilheteria*	e(r) bil-yetteree'e(r)
the train	*o comboio*	oo kohmboy'oo
a travelling rug	*uma manta de viajem*	oom'e(r) mun'te(r) di vee*i*'zhe*n*(*g*)
the trunk	*o bahú*	oo bah-oo'
the voyage	*a viagem*	e(r) vee*i*'zhe*n*(*g*)
the waiter	*o môço de servir*	oo moh'soo di serr'veer
the waiting-room	*a sala de espera*	e(r) sahle(r) di ishpair'e(r)
the whip	*o chicote*	oo sheekaw'ti

24. Countries and Nations. *(Paizes e Nações.)*

English.	Portuguese.	Pronunciation.
Africa	*a Africa*	e(r) ah'frike(r)
America	*a America*	e(r) um-er'rike(r)
an American	*um Americano*	oon(g) um-errikun'oo
Asia	*a Asia*	e(r) ah'zi-e(r)
Australia	*a Australia*	e(r) owshtrah'li-e(r)
Austria	*a Austria*	e(r) owsh'tri-e(r)
an Austrian	*um Austriaco*	oon(g) owshtree'e(r)koo
a Belgian	*um Belga*	oon(g) bel'ghe(r)
Belgium	*a Belgica*	e(r) bel'zhike(r)
Bohemia	*a Bohemia*	e(r) boo-em'i-e(r)
Brazil	*o Brazil*	oo bre(r)zeel'
a Brazilian	*um Brazileiro*	oon(g) bre(r)zeelay'roo
Canada	*o Canadá*	oo kunne(r)dah'
Cuba	*a Cuba*	e(r) koo'be(r)
a Dane	*um Dinamarquez*	oon(g) deene(r)murrkezh'
Denmark	*a Dinamarca*	e(r) deene(r)mahr'ke(r)
a Dutchman	*um Hollandez*	oon(g) awlundezh'
the East Indies	*as Indias Orientes*	uz een'di-uzh awrient'izh
the empire	*o imperio*	oo eempair'ioo
England	*a Inglaterra*	e(r) een(g)gle(r)tair're(r)
an Englishman	*um Inglez*	oon(g) een(g)glezh'
Europe	*a Europa*	e(r) eh-ooraw'pe(r)
a European	*um Europeo*	oon(g) eh-ooroopeh'oo
France	*a França*	e(r) frun(g)'se(r)
a Frenchman	*um Francez*	oon(g) frun(g)sezh'
a German	*um Allemão*	oon(g) ullimown(g)'
Germany	*a Allemanha*	e(r) ullimun'ye(r)
Greece	*a Grecia*	e(r) gress'i-e(r)
a Greek	*um Grego*	oon(g) greg'oo
Holland	*a Hollanda*	e(r) aw-lun'de(r)
Hungary	*a Hungria*	e(r) oon(g)-gree'e(r)
Ireland	*a Irlanda*	oon(g) eerlun'de(r)
an Irishman	*um Irlandez*	oon(g) eerlundezh'
an Italian	*um Italiano*	oon(g) eetul-ee-un'oo
Italy	*a Italia*	e(r) eetah'li-e(r)
Japan	*o Japão*	oo zhe(r)pown(g)'
a Japanese	*um Japonez*	oon(g) zhe(r)poonezh'
the kingdom	*o reino*	oo ray'noo

English.	Portuguese.	Pronunciation.
Lisbon	*Lisboa*	leezhboh'e(r)
an inhabitant of Lisbon	*um habitante de Lisboa*	oon(g) e(r)bitun'ti di leezhboh'e(r)
London	*Londres*	lohn'drizh
Norway	*a Noruega*	e(r) noorooeh'ghe(r)
a Norwegian	*um Noruguez*	oon(g) noorooeh-gezh'
Russia	*Portugal*	poortoogahl'
a Russian	*um Portuguez*	oon(g) poortoogezh'
Portugal	*a Russia*	e(r) roo'si-e(r)
a Portuguese	*um Russo*	oon(g) roos'soo
a Scotchman	*um Escocez*	oon(g) ishkoosezh'
Scotland	*a Escocia*	e(r) ishkaw'si-e(r)
Spain	*a Hespanha*	e(r) ishpun'ye(r)
a Spaniard	*um Hespanhol*	oon(g) ishpun-yawl'
a Swede	*um Sueco*	oon(g) soo-ek'oo
Sweden	*a Suecia*	e(r) soo-ess'i-e(r)
a Swiss	*um Suisso*	oon(g) soo-ees'soo
Switzerland	*a Suissa*	e(r) soo-ees'se(r)
a Turk	*um Turco*	oon(g) toor'koo
Turkey	*a Turquia*	e(r) toorkee'e(r)
the United States	*os Estados Unidos*	ooz ishtah'dooz oonee'-doozh
the West Indies	*as Antilhas*	uz un-teel'yuzh

25. Commercial and Trading Terms.

(Termos Commerciaes e de Negocios.)

(For Conversations see pp. 117 & 118.)

Account, to settle an	*saldar uma conta*	sahldahr' oom'e(r) kohn'-te(r)
—, to close	*fechar uma conta*	fishar' oom'e(r) kohn'-te(r)
—, current	*conta-corrente*	kohn'te(r) koorren'ti
—, joint	*— commum*	— koommoon(g)'
— of sale	*— de venda*	— di vend'e(r)
an acknowledgment	*um reconhecimento*	oon(g) rikoon-yessiment'oo
an advance (of money)	*um adiantamento (de dinheiro)*	oon(g) e(r)di-unte(r)-ment'oo di din-yay'roo
advice, letter of	*carta* (f.) *de aviso*	kahr'te(r) di e(r)vee'zoo
the agency	*a agencia*	e(r) e(r)zhen(g)'see-e(r)
the agent	*o agente*	oo e(r)zhen'ti
the apprentice	*o aprendiz*	oo e(r)prendeezh'
the arrangement	*o accôrdo*	oo ukkohr'doo

English.	Portuguese.	Pronunciation.
arrear, in	*em atrazo*	ain(*g*) ut-rah'zoo
the assets	*o activo*	oo ahtee'voo
authorize, to	*autorizar*	owtoorizahr'
the average	*a avaria*	e(r) uvvur-ee'e(r)
the balance	*o saldo*	oo sahl'doo
— — of account	*— — de contas*	— — di kohn'tuzh
— — -sheet	*o balanço*	oo be(r)lun(*g*)'soo
the bank	*o banco*	oo bun(*g*)'koo
the bearer [tion	*o portador*	oo poorte(r)dohr' [vohr'
bill, an accommoda-	*uma letra de favor*	oom'e(r) let're(r) di fe(r)-
a bill at sight	*— — á vista*	— — ah veesh'te(r)
— — at three months' date	*— — a tres mezes da data*	— — e(r) trezh mez'izh de(r) dah'te(r)
— — of lading	*um conhecimento*	oon(*g*) koon-yissimen'too
bond, in	*captivo na alfandega*	kahteev'oo ne(r) ahlfun'-di-gher
the bonded goods	*as mercadorias captivas na alfandega*	uzh merrke(r)doo-ree'uzh kahtee'vuzh ne(r) ahl-fun'di-ghe(r)
the book-keeper	*o guarda-livros*	oo gwahr'de(r)-leev'roozh
the brokerage	*a corretagem*	e(r) koorriti'zhen(*g*) [yoo
business, the retail	*o negocio, a retalho*	oo nigaw'sioo, e(r) riti'l-
—, the wholesale	*— —, por atacado*	— — poor utte(r)kah'doo
the buyer	*o comprador*	oo kohmpre(r)dohr'
carriage- (post-) paid	*transporte pago, franqueado*	trun(*g*)shpawr'ti pah'goo, frun(*g*)ki-ah'doo
the cartage	*o carreto*	oo kurret'oo
the catalogue	*o catalogo*	oo ke(r)tahl'oogoo
charter a ship, to	*fretar um navio*	fritahr' oon(*g*) ne(r)vee'oo
claim, to send in a	*apresentar uma reclamação*	up-riz-entahr' oom'e(r) ri-klum-e(r)sown(*g*)'
—, to make good a	*justificar — —*	zhoostifikahr' — —
the clearing-house (customs)	*a casa de despacho (alfandega)*	e(r)kah'ze(r) di dispah'-shoo [ahlfun'di-ghe(r)]
the clerk	*o caixero*	oo ki-shai'roo
company, a joint-stock	*uma sociedade anonyma*	oom'e(r) soosi-ehdah'di un-awn'eem-e(r)
—, a limited	*— — de responsabilidade limitada*	— — di rishpohnse(r)-bilidah'di limitah'de(r)
the complaint	*a queixa*	e(r) kay'she(r)

English.	Portuguese.	Pronunciation.
the contract	*o contrato*	oo kohntrah'too
cost, insurance and freight (c.i.f.)	*custo, frete e seguro* (*c.f.s.*) m.	koosh'too, fret'i i sigoo'-roo
a credit balance	*um saldo a credito*	oon(*g*) sahl'doo e(r) kred'-itoo
a creditor	*um crédor*	oon(*g*) kreh-dohr'
the custom-house	*a alfandega*	e(r) ahlfun'di-ghe(r)
the customs' duties	*os direitos da alfandega*	oozh diray'toozh de(r) ahlfun'di-ghe(r)
the damages, compensation	*os damnos, a compensação*	oozh dun'noozh, e(r) kohmpen(*g*)se(r)sown(*g*)'
damages, to claim	*reclamar damnos*	rikle(r)mahr' dun'noozh
date, at three months'	*a tres mezes da data*	e(r) trezh mez'izh de(r) dah'te(r)
debit and credit	*debito e credito* m.	deb'itoo i kred'itoo
the debtor	*o devedor*	oo devvidohr'
deliver, to	*entregar*	intrigahr'
delivered free	*entregue franco*	intreh'ghi frun(*g*)'koo
the demurrage	*a detenção*	e(r) di-ten(*g*)sown(*g*)'
the director	*o director*	oo diraytohr'
the discount	*o desconto*	oo dishkohn'too
discount, to	*discontar*	dishkohntahr'
the dividend warrant	*cautella de titulo a dividendos*	kowtel'le(r) di tee'tooloo e(r) dividen'doozh
dock and harbour dues	*direitos do dique e do porto*	diray'toozh doo dee'ki i doo pohr'too
double entry	*lançamento* (m.) *duplo*	lun(*g*)se(r)men'too doo'-ploo
the drawer (of bill)	*o sacador*	oo se(r)-ke(r)-dohr'
duty, export	*direitos* (m.pl.) *de exportação*	diray'toozh di ishpoor-tussown(*g*)'
— -free	*livre de direitos*	leev'ri di diray'toozh
—, import	*direitos de importação*	diray'toozh di impoor-tussowng'
—, liable to	*sugeito a direitos*	soozhay'too e(r) diray'-toozh
enclosed	*junt-o* m., *-a* f.	zhoon't-oo, -e(r)
the enclosure	*inclus-o* m., *-a* f.	een(*g*)klooz'-oo, -e(r)
endorse, to	*endossar*	indoossahr'
the endorsement	*o endosse*	oo indaw'si
the exchange	*o cambio*	oo kum'bioo
the firm	*a firma*	e(r) feer'me(r)
forwarding	*expedição* f.	ishpidisown(*g*)'

English.	Portuguese.	Pronunciation.
the forwarding agent	*o agente de expedições*	oo e(r)zhen'ti di ishpidisoy'*n*(*g*)zh
free on board (f.o.b.)	*livre abordo*	lee'vri e(r)bohr'doo
gross weight	*peso bruto*	pez'oo broo'too
the guarantee	*a garantia*	e(r) gurruntee'e(r)
the guarantor	*o fiador*	oo fee-e(r)dohr'
an I.O.U.	*um pagarei*	oo*n*(*g*) puggurray'
import and export	*importação e exportação*	impoorte(r)sow*n*(*g*)' i ishpoorte(r)sow*n*(*g*)'
the information	*a informação*	e(r) ee*n*(*g*)foormus-sow*ng*'
inquire, to	*indagar*	eende(r)gahr'
the inquiry	*a pergunta*	e(r) perrgoon'te(r)
insurance, marine	*seguro* (m.) *maritimo*	sigoo'roo murree'timoo
— broker	*corretor* (m.) *de seguros*	koorretohr' di sigoo'roozh
— company	*companhia* (f.) — —	kohmpun-yee'e(r) di sigoo'roozh
— policy	*apolice* (f.) *de seguro*	e(r)pawl'si di sigoo'roo
— premium	*premio* (m.) — —	prem'ioo di sigoo'roo
insure against, to	*effectuar o seguro contra*	iffet-ooahr' oo sigoo'roo kohn'tre(r)
interest, the rate of	*a taxa de juros*	e(r) tah'she(r) di zhoo'roozh
the introduction	*a apresentação*	e(r) up-rizentussow*n*(*g*)'
the landing charges	*as despezas de desembarque*	uzh dishpeh'zuzh di disimbahr'ki
the liabilities	*o passivo*	oo pus-see'voo
the lighterage	*a descarga em lanchas*	e(r) dishkahr'ghe(r) ai*n*(*g*) lu*n*(*g*)'shuzh
load, to	*carregar*	kurrigahr'
the loss	*o prejuizo*	oo pri-zhooee'zoo
the manager	*o gerente*	oo zherren'ti
market	*mercado* m.	merrkah'doo
—, the cattle	*o mercado de gado*	oo merrkah'doo di gah'doo
—, the foreign	— — *estrangeiro*	— — ishtru*n*(*g*)zhay'roo
—, the home	— — *nacional*	— — nussioonahl'
—, the London	— — *de Londres*	— — di lohn'drizh
—, the meat	— — *de carne*	— — di kahr'ni
the market-day	*o dia de mercado*	oo dee'e(r) di merrkah'doo
the market dues	*os impostos do mercado*	ooz impohsh'toozh doo merrkah'doo

English.	Portuguese.	Pronunciation.
the market price	*o preço do mercado*	oo pres'soo doo merrkah'doo
negotiable, saleable	*negociavel, vendavel*	nigooseeah'vel, vendah'vel
offer (for sale), to	*offerecer*	awfferressehr'
the offers	*as offertas*	uz awffair'tuzh
order, to	*encommendar*	ee*n*(*g*)koommendahr'
the packing	*a emballagem*	e(r) imbe(r)lli'zhe*n*(*g*)
the partnership	*a sociedade*	e(r) soosi-eh-dah'di
payable at sight	*pagavel á vista*	pe(r)gah'vel ah veesh'te(r)
the port of delivery	*o porto de entrega*	oo pohr'too di intreg'e(r)
price, the cost-	*o preço do custo*	oo press'oo doo koosh'too
— -list	*lista* (f.) *de preços*	leesh'te(r) di press'oozh
—, the selling	*o preço de venda*	oo press'oo di ven'de(r)
—, the wholesale	*— — por atacado*	— — poor utte(r)kah'doo
the quotation (of price)	*a cotação*	e(r) koote(r)sow*n*(*g*)'
—, the lowest	*— — mais baixa*	— — mi'zh bi'she(r)
the receipt	*o recibo*	oo rissee'boo
the reduction	*o abatimento*	oo e(r)but-iment'oo
register, to	*registar*	rizh-ishtahr'
a registered letter	*uma carta registada*	oom'er kahr'te(r) rizhishtah'de(r)
the registered tonnage	*as tonelladas de registro*	uzh toonellah'duzh di rizheesh'troo
the registration	*o registro*	oo rizheesh'troo
— — fee	*o direito de registro*	oo diray'too di rizheesh'troo
the rent	*a renda*	e(r) ren'de(r)
the representative	*o representante*	oo ripriz-entun'ti
a salesman (seller)	*um vendedor*	oo*n*(*g*) vendidohr'
the settling days	*os dias de liquidação*	oozh dee'uzh di leekidussow*n*(*g*)'
shares	*acções* f.pl.	ahssoy'*n*(*g*)zh
—, debenture	*obrigações* f.pl.	awbrigussoy'*n*(*g*)zh
—, preference	*acções de preferencia*	ahssoy'*n*(*g*)zh di priferren(*g*)'see-e(r)
—, railway	*— do caminho de ferro*	— doo ke(r)meen'yoo di fair'roo
ship, to	*embarcar*	imburrkahr'
a speculator	*um especulador*	oo*n*(*g*) ishpikoole(r)dohr'
a ship-broker	*um corretor de navios*	oo*n*(*g*) koorretohr' di ne(r)vee'oozh
the shipping charges	*as despezas de embarque*	uzh dishpeh'zuzh di imbahr'ki

English.	Portuguese.	Pronunciation.
the shipping house	*a casa expedidora*	e(r) kah'ze(r) ishpidi-
solvent	*solvente*	sawlvent'i [dawr'e(r)
the stock	*os fundos*	oozh foon'doozh [doozh
the stock-broker	*o corretor de fundos*	oo koorretohr' di foon'-
the stowage	*a arrumação da carga*	e(r) urroome(r)sown(g)' de(r) kahr'ghe(r)
the telegraphic address	*o endereço telegraphico* [*bóque*	oo inderress'oo tilligrah'fikoo [baw'ki
the towing charges	*as despezas de re-*	uzh dishpez'uzh di ri-
the trade	*o negocio*	oo nigaw'sioo
the underwriter	*o segurador*	oo sigoore(r)dohr'
the unloading	*a descarga*	e(r) dishkahr'ghe(r)
the wharf	*o caes trapiche*	oo ki'zh tre(r)peesh'i
the wharfage	*os direitos de caes*	oozh diray'toozh di ki'zh
wholesale	*por atacado*	poor utte(r)kah'doh
the winding-up	*a liquidação*	e(r) leeki-de(r)sown(g)'

26. Cycling. (*Velocipedismo.*)

(For Conversations see pp. 113 & 114.)

English.	Portuguese.	Pronunciation.
The axle	*o eixo*	oo ay'shoo [luzh
the ball bearings	*os mancaes de bolas*	oozh munki'zh di baw'-
the bell	*a campaínha*	e(r) kumpe(r)een'ye(r)
the bicycle	*o bicycleta*	e(r) beesiklet'te(r)
the brake	*o travão*	oo tre(r)vown(g)'
the cement	*o cimento*	oo seemen'too
the chain	*a corrente*	e(r) koorren'ti
chainless	*sem corrente*	sain(g) koorren'ti
the chain-wheel	*a roda da corrente*	e(r) raw'de(r) de(r) koor-
the cone	*o cone*	oo kaw'ni [ren'ti
the connection	*a connexão*	e(r) koonnexown(g)'
the crank	*a manivela*	e(r) munnivel'le(r)
the cyclist	*o* (m.) / *a* (f.) *bicyclista*	oo / e(r) beesikleesh'te(r)
a cycling race	*uma corrida de bicycletas*	oom'e(r) koorree'de(r) di beesiklet'uzh
a cycling track	*um trilho de bicycletas*	oon(g) treel'yoo di beesiklet'uzh
a cyclometer	*um cyclometro*	oon(g) seeklaw'mitroo
dismount, to	*apear*	e(r)piahr'
electro-plate, to	*nickelar*	neekilahr'

English.	Portuguese.	Pronunciation.
the enamel	*o esmalte*	oo izhmahl'ti
the foot-step	*o estribo*	oo ishtree'boo
the fork	*o garfo*	oo gahr'foo
the frame	*a armação*	e(r) ahrmussow*n*(*g*)'
the friction	*a fricção*	e(r) freeksow*n*(*g*)'
the gear, gearing	*as multiplicações* [*grande*	uzh mooltiplikkus-soy'*n*(*g*)zh [grun'di
gear, high	*a multiplicação*	e(r) mooltiplikussow*n*(*g*)'
—, low	— — *pequena*	— — pi-ken'e(r)
the gear-case	*a capa da cadeia*	e(r) kah'pe(r) de(r) ke(r)-
geared to ...	*ligado*	leegah'doo [day'e(r)
the handles (grips)	*os punhos do guiador*	oozh poon'yoozh doo ghee-e(r)dohr'
the handle bar	*o guiador*	oo ghee-e(r)dohr'
the hub	*a capa do eixo*	e(r) kah'pe(r) doo ay'shoo
the indiarubber	*a gomma elastica* [*racha*	e(r) goh'me(r) ilahsh'-tike(r) [she(r)
— — solution	*o remendo de bor-*	oo rimen'doo di boorah'-
the knapsack	*a mochila*	e(r) mooshee'le(r)
the lamp	*a lanterna*	e(r) lun-tair'ne(r) [ne(r)
the lamp bracket	*o porta-lanterna*	oo pawr'te(r)-lun-tair'-
the lamp wick [ois)	*a torcida da lanterna*	e(r) toorsee'de(r) der lun-tair'ne(r)
the leather (cham-	*a camurça*	e(r) kum-oor'se(r)
a link	*un ello*	oo*n*(*g*) el'loo
the lubricator	*o lubricador*	oo loobrike(r)dohr'
— — protector	*o guarda-lubricador*	oo gwahr'de(r)-loobri-ke(r)dohr'
the luggage-carrier	*o porta-bagagem; a mala*	oo pawr'te(r) be(r)ghi'-zhe*n*(*g*); e(r) mah'le(r)
map	*o mappa*	oo mahp'pe(r)
mount, to	*montar*	mohntahr'
the mudguard	*o guarda-lâma*	oo gwahr'de(r)-lum'e(r)
the nut	*a porca*	e(r) pawr'ke(r) [ne(r)
the oil for burning	*o azeite de lanterna*	oo uzzay'ti di lun-tair'-
—.— for lubricating	— — *de lubricar*	— — di loobrikahr'
the oil can	*a almotolia*	e(r) ahlmootoolee'e(r)
the pedal	*o pedal*	oo pidahl' [dahl'
the pedal brake	*o travão do pedal*	oo tre(r)vow*n*(*g*)' doo pi-
pedal rubber	*borracha* (f.) *do pedal*	boorrah'she(r) doo pidahl'

English.	Portuguese.	Pronunciation.
the pump	*a bomba*	e(r) bohm'be(r)
the pump tube	*o tubo da bomba*	oo too'boo de(r) bohm'be(r)
pump up, to	*encher os pneumaticos*	in(*g*)shehr' oozh neh-oomah'tikoozh
rags, some old	*uns trapos velhos*	oon(*g*)zh trah'poozh vel'yoozh
removable	*de tirar e pôr*	di teerahr' i pohr
the repairing outfit	*os sobrecellentes para reparos*	oozh soobrisellen'tizh pur're(r) ripahr'oozh
the rim	*a camba*	e(r) kum'be(r)
the rim-brake	*o travão da camba*	oo tre(r)vown(*g*)' der kum'be(r)
the saddle	*o sellim*	oo silleen(*g*)'
the saddle bag	*o alforge*	oo ahlfawr'zhi
the saddle pillar	*o espigão do sellim*	oo ishpigown(*g*)' doo silleen(*g*)'
a screw	*um parafuzo*	oon(*g*) purre(r)foo'zoo
a screw-bolt of chain	*uma tarracha da corrente*	oom'e(r) turrah'she(r) de(r) koorren'ti
screw, to	*aparafuzar*	e(r)purre(r)foozahr'
the spanner	*a chave de porcas*	e(r) shah'vi di pawr'kuzh
the spokes	*os raios*	oozh ri'oozh
the spring	*a mola*	e(r) maw'le(r)
start off, to	*partir*	purrteer'
steer, to	*guiar*	ghi-ahr'
the strap (leather)	*a corrêa*	e(r) koorrai'e(r)
take to pieces, to	*desmanchar*	dizhmun(*g*)shahr'
tighten up, to	*apertar*	e(r)purrtahr'
a toe clip	*um gancho dos pedaes*	oon(*g*) gun(*g*)'shoo doozh pidi'zh
a tricycle	*uma tricycleta*	oom'e(r) tree-si-klet'e(r)
the trousers' clip	*o gancho para prender as calças*	oo gun(*g*)'shoo purre(r) prendehr' uzh kahl'suzh
the tube, inner	*o tubo interior*	oo too'boo intirriohr'
the tube (outer cover)	*a capa exterior do tubo*	e(r) kah'pe(r) ishtirriohr' doo too'boo
tyre (pneumatic)	*pneumatico* m.	neh-oomah'tikoo
unscrew, to	*desparafuzar*	dizhpurre(r)foozahr'
the valve	*a valvula*	e(r) vahl'voole(r)
the valve tube	*o tubo da valvula*	oo too'boo de(r) vahl'voole(r)
the wallet	*a maleta*	e(r) mullet'e(r)
wheel, the front	*a roda dianteira*	e(r) raw'de(r) di-untay're(r)
—, the back	— — *trazeira*	— — truzzay're(r)

27. Motoring Terms. (*Termos Automobiliaros.*)

(See also Cycling, pp. 51 & 113, and Motoring, p. 115.)

English.	Portuguese.	Pronunciation.
Accumulator	*accumulador* m.	e(r)koomoolle(r)dohr'
a battery	*uma bateria*	oom'e(r) be(r)terree'e(r)
the brake collar (steel)	*a gola de aço do travão*	e(r) gaw'le(r) di ah'soo doo tre(r)vown(g)'
the cam	*a roda dentada*	e(r) raw'de(r) dentah'-
the carburator	*o carburador*	oo kurboore(r)dohr' [de(r)
the chain adjust-	*a liga da cadeia*	e(r) lee'ghe(r) de(r) ke(r)-
the claw [ment	*a garra*	e(r) gahr're(r) [day'e(r)
the contact breaker (trembler)	*o tremulador*	oo trimoole(r)dohr'
the driver	*o machinista*	oo me(r)kineesh'te(r)
the elbow	*o cotovello*	oo kootoovel'loo
electrical	*electric-o* m., *-a* f.	i-let'rik-oo, -e(r)
the electricity	*a electricidade*	e(r) i-letrissidah'di
the exhaust-box (silencer)	*o silenciador*	oo seelen(g)si-e(r)dohr' [goh'too
the exhaust-valve	*a valvula de esgoto*	e(r) vahl'voole(r) di izh-
the fly-wheel	*a roda volante*	e(r) raw'de(r) voolun'ti
the handle (start-	*a manivela*	e(r) munnivel'e(r) [loozh
horse-power [ing)	*força de cavallos*	fohr'se(r) di ke(r)vahl'-
ignition	*ignição* f.	eegneessown(g)' [un'ke(r)
the lever (handle)	*a mão da alavanca*	e(r) mown(g) de(r) ul-uv-
the lever	*a alavanca*	e(r) ul-uv-un'ke(r)
the motor	*o motor*	oo mootohr'
petrol, some	*algum petroleo*	ahlgoon(g)' pitraw'lioo
the pinion	*a cavilha*	e(r) kuv-eel'ye(r)
the rack	*o cavallete*	oo kuv-ullet'i
the reservoir	*o deposito* [*ceder*	oo dipaw'zitoo [sidehr'
the reversing gear	*o apparelho de retro-*	oo uppurrel'yoo di ritroo-
speed, high	*alta velocidade*	ahl'te(r) vilossidah'di
—, low	*baixa* —	bi'she(r) —
the speed-changing gear	*o apparelho de mudar a velocidade*	oo uppurrel'yoo di moodahr' e(r) vilossidah'di
the starting gear	*o apparelho de partida*	oo uppurrel'yoo di purrtee'de(r)
the steering bar	*o braço do apparelho de guiar*	oo brah'soo doo uppurrel'yoo di ghi-ahr'
the tap	*a torneira*	e(r) toorrnay're(r)

28. Photography. *(Photographia.)*

(For Conversations, see p. 116.)

English.	Portuguese.	Pronunciation.
Backgrounds	*fundos*	foon'doozh
—, cloth	*panno do fundo*	pun'noo doo foon'doo
backing paper	*papel do fundo*	pe(r)pel' doo foon'doo
the camera	*a camera escura*	e(r) kum'urre(r) ish-koo're(r)
dark slide (double)	*caixilho escuro (dobrado)*	ki-sheel'yoo ishkoo'roo (doobrah'doo)
dishes for developing	*terrinas para revelar*	terreen'uzh pur're(r) revelahr'
— for fixing	— — *fixar*	— — feexahr'
the draining rack	*o escorredouro*	oo ishkoorridoh'roo
dry plates	*clichês seccos*	kleeshayzh' sek'koozh
the exposure	*a exposição*	e(r) ishpoozisown(g)'
the film	*o pelliculo*	oo pelleek'ooloo
the focus	*o foco*	oo faw'koo
focussing glasses	*lentes de enfocar*	lent'izh di in(g)fookahr'
the funnels	*os funis*	oozh fooneezh'
a glass measure	*uma medida de* [*vidro*	oom'e(r) midee'de(r) di [vee'droo
a half-plate	*uma semi-cliché*	oom'e(r) semi-kleeshay'
iris diaphragms	*diaphragma iris*	dee-e(r)frahg'me(r) ee'-rizh
lamp, a dark-room	*uma lanterna rôxa*	oom'e(r) lun-tair'ne(r) [roh'she(r)
lamps, flash	*lanternas de relam-* [*piar*	lun-tair'nuzh di rilum- [peeahr'
the lens	*a lente*	e(r) len'ti
the mount	*a armação*	e(r) urrmussown(g)'
the plate-holder	*o porta-cliché*	oo pohr'te(r)-kleeshay'
the plate-lifter	*as tenazes*	uzh tenahz'izh
platinotypes	*platinotypos*	plahtinooteep'oozh
print, to	*imprimir*	eemprimeer'
the printing	*o impresso*	oo eempres'soo
— — frame	*a forma de inprimir*	e(r) fawr'me(r) di eem-primeer'
scales and weights	*balanças e pesos*	be(r)lun(g)'suz i pez'ooz
the shutter	*o tapadeiro*	oo te(r)pe(r)day'roo
—, time and instantaneous	— — *temporaneo e instantaneo*	— — tempoo-run'ioo i in(g)shtuntun'ioo
the speed indicator	*o indicador da velocidade*	oo eendeeke(r)dohr' de(r) vilossidah'di

English.	Portuguese.	Pronunciation.
squeegees with solid rubber roller	*lambazes com rôlo solido de borracha*	lum-bah'zizh koon(*g*) roh'loo saw'lidoo di boorrah'she(r)
tripod (two-fold)	*tripode (duplo)*	oo tree'poodi (doo'ploo)
the view-finder	*o vizador*	oo veeze(r)dohr'
— —, square	*vista quadrada*	veesh'te(r) kwudrah'de(r)
— —, oblong	*vista oblonga*	— awblawn(*g*)'ghe(r)
washing tanks	*tanques para lavagem*	tun'kizh pur're(r) luv-*i*'zhen(*g*)

29. Amusements. *(Recreios.)*

A ball	*um baile*	oon(*g*) b*i*'li
a circus	*um circo*	oon(*g*) seer'koo
a concert	*um concerto*	oon(*g*) kohn(*g*)sair'too
the accompanist [ment	*o acompunhador*	oo e(r)kohmpun-ye(r)-dohr' [men'too
the accompani-	*o acompanhamento*	oo e(r)kohmpun-ye(r)-
the brass band	*a banda*	e(r) bun'de(r)
the chorus	*o côro*	oo koh'roo [tre(r)
the conductor	*o chefe da orchestra*	oo shef'i de(r) awrkesh'-
the drum	*o tambor*	oo tumbohr' [toozh
the instruments	*os instrumentos*	ooz in(*g*)shtroomen'-
the brass —	*— — de metal*	— — di mit-ahl'
the string —	*— — de corda*	— — di kohr'de(r)
the orchestra	*a orchestra*	e(r) awrkesh'tre(r)
the pianist	*o (a) pianista*, m. & f.	oo [e(r)] peeun-eesh'te(r)
the piano	*o piano*	oo peeun'oo
the recital	*a recita*	e(r) risee'te(r)
a singer	*um cantor* (m.), *uma cantora* (f.)	oon(*g*) kuntohr', oom'e(r) kuntawr'e(r)
a trumpet	*o clarim*	oo klurreen(*g*)'
a violin	*uma rabeca*	oom'e(r) re(r)bek'e(r)
the exhibition	*a exposição*	e(r) ispoozisown(*g*)'
the flower-show	*— — de flores*	— — di floh'rezh
the museum	*o museo*	oo moozeh'oo
the music-hall	*o theatro de variedades*	oo tiah'troo di vurrieh-dah'dizh
the opera	*a opera*	e(r) aw'perre(r) [re(r)
the opera-house	*o theatro da opera*	oo tiah'troo de(r) aw'per-

English.	Portuguese.	Pronunciation.
the picture gallery	*a galeria de quadros*	e(r) gullurree'e(r) di kwah'droozh
the theatre	*o theatro*	oo tiah'troo
the act	*o acto*	oo ahk'too
the actor	*o actor*	oo ahtohr'
the actress	*a actriz*	e(r) ahtreezh'
the auditorium	*o auditorio*	oo owditaw'rioo
the ballet	*o baile de espectaculo*	oo bi'li di ishpet-ah'koo-loo
the band	*a banda*	e(r) bun'de(r)
the box-office	*o camaroteiro*	oo kummurrootay'roo
the cloak-room	*a casa de guarda-roupa*	e(r) kah'ze(r) di gwahr'-de(r)roh'pe(r)
the comedian	*o comico*	oo kaw'mikoo
the comedy	*a comedia*	e(r) koomed'ie(r)
the curtain	*a cortina*	e(r) koortee'ne(r)
the dancer	*o bailarino* (m.), *a bailarina* (f.)	oo bi-lurree'noo, e(r) bi-lurree'ne(r)
the footlights	*a fileira de luzes scenicas*	e(r) feelay're(r) di loo'zizh sen'ikuzh
the manager	*o director*	oo diraytohr'
the play	*a peça*	e(r) pes'se(r)
the programme	*o programma*	oo proogrum'me(r)
the prompter	*o ponto*	oo pohn'too
the proprietor	*o proprietario*	oo prooprieh-tah'rioo
the refreshment-room	*o salão de refrescos*	oo sullown(g)' di rifresh'-koozh
the scene	*a scena*	e(r) sen'ne(r)
the seats	*os assentos*	ooz us-sen'toozh
the boxes	*os camarotes*	oozh kummur-aw'tizh
the dress circle	*o balcão de primeira ordem*	oo bahlkown(g)' di prim-ay're(r) awr'den(g)
the gallery	*a galeria*	e(r) gulleree'e(r)
the pit	*a platêa*	e(r) ple(r)tay'e(r)
the reserved seats	*os lugares reservados*	oozh loogah'rizh rez-ehr-vah'doozh
the stalls	*os fauteuils de orchestra*	oozh fohtay'zh di awr-kesh'tre(r)
the stage	*o palco*	oo pahl'koo
— — manager	*o contra-regra*	oo kohn'tre(r)-reg're(r)
the tickets	*os bilhetes*	oozh beel-yet'izh

English.	Portuguese.	Pronunciation.
the theatre (*cont.*)		
the tragedy	*a tragedia*	e(r) tre(r)zhed'i-e(r)
the tragedian	*o actor tragico*	oo ahtohr' trah'zhikoo
sports and games	*o "sport" e jôgos*	oo spawrt i zhoh'goozh
assault-at-arms	*torneio* (m.) *de exercicios militares*	toornay'oo di ezzerrsee'sioozh militah'rizh
billiards (to play)	*jogar ao bilhar*	zhoogahr' ah'oo beel-yahr'
the boxing match	*o desafio de sôcco*	oo diz-e(r)fee'oo di soh'-koh
chess	*xadrez*	she(r)drezh'
cricket	*cricket*	krik'it
draughts	*damas*	dum'uzh
the grand-stand	*a tribuna mór*	e(r) treeboo'ne(r) mawr
the jockey	*o jockey*	oo zhaw'ki
the match	*o desafio*	oo diz-e(r)fee'oo
polo	*jogo da péla (polo)*	zhoh'goo de(r) pel'e(r) (polo)
the races	*as corridas de cavallos*	uzh koorree'duzh di ke(r)vahl'loozh
the race-course	*o terreno de corridas*	oo terrain'oo di koorree'duzh
tennis	*tennis*	tennis

30. Correspondence. *(A Correspondencia.)*

(For Conversations see page 100.)

English.	Portuguese.	Pronunciation.
The address	*o endereço*	oo inderres'soo
blotting-paper	*papel de mata-borrão*	pe(r)pel' di mah'te(r)-boorrown(*g*)'
the book	*o livro*	oo lee'vroo
the date	*a data*	e(r) dah'te(r)
an enclosure	*um incluzo* (m.), *uma incluza* (f.)	oon(*g*) in(*g*)kloo'zoo, oom'e(r) in(*g*)kloo'ze(r)
an envelope	*um sobrescripto*	oon(*g*) sohbrishkree'too
herewith	*aqui junt-o, -a*	e(r)kee' zhoon't-oo, -e(r)
immediate	*urgente*	oorzhen'ti
the ink	*a tinta*	e(r) teen'te(r)
the inkstand	*o tinteiro*	oo teentay'roo
the letter	*a carta*	e(r) kahr'te(r)
— — -box	*a caixa de cartas*	e(r) ki'she(r) di kahr'tuzh
— — -card	*o bilhete postal*	oo beel-yet'i pooshtahl'
the note	*a cartinha*	e(r) kurrteen'ye(r)

English.	Portuguese.	Pronunciation.
the note-paper	*o papel formato pequeno*	oo pe(r)pel' foormah'too peeken'oo
the paper	*o papel*	oo pe(r)pel' [soo
a pen, steel (nib)	*uma penna de aço*	oom'e(r) pen'ne(r) di ah'-
— —, fountain	*— — inesgotavel*	— — in-izhgootah'vel
— — -holder	*uma caneta*	oom'e(r) ke(r)net'e(r)
a pencil	*um lapis*	oo*n*(*g*) lah'pizh
a penknife	*um canivete*	oo*n*(*g*) kunnivet'i
a quire	*um caderno*	oo*n*(*g*) ke(r)dair'noo
the scissors	*a tezoura*	e(r) tizoh're(r) [boo
the seal	*o sello, o carimbo*	oo sel'loo, oo kurreem'-
the sealing-wax	*o lacre de sellar*	oo lah'kri di sellahr'
a sheet (of paper)	*uma folha de papel*	oom'e(r) fohl'ye(r) di pe(r)pel'
the signature	*a assignatura*	e(r) us-seene(r)too're(r)
the writing	*o escripto*	oo ishkree'too
— — -desk	*a escrivaninha*	e(r) ishkrivun-een'ye(r)
— — materials	*os materiaes para escrever*	oozh me(r)terri-*i*'zh pur'-re(r) ishkrivehr'

31. Post-office and Telegrams.

(O Correio e Telegrammas.)

(For Conversations see page 101.)

English.	Portuguese.	Pronunciation.
Book post	*correio* (m.) *de im-*	koorray'oo di impres'-
the counterfoil	*o talão* [*pressos*	oo tullow*n*(*g*)' [soozh
the description	*a descripção*	e(r) dishkreesow*n*(*g*)'
the despatch-note	*a nota de despacho*	e(r) naw'te(r) di dishpah'-
the destination	*o destino*	oo dishtee'noo [shoo
the excess postage	*o porte em excesso*	oo pawr'ti ai*n*(*g*) ishses'-soo
the insured value	*o valor seguro*	oo ve(r)lohr' sigoo'roo
letter post	*correio de cartas*	koorray'oo di kahr'tuzh
a money order	*um vale do correio*	oo*n*(*g*) vah'li doo koor-ray'oo
	[*theúdo*	[tioo'doo
nature of contents	*natureza do con-*	ne(r)toorez'e(r) doo kohn-
a newspaper wrapper	*um envoltorio de jornaes*	oo*n*(*g*) i*n*(*g*)vawltaw'rioo di zhoorn*i*'zh
the number	*o numero*	oo noo'merroo
parcel post	*correio de encommendas*	koorray'oo di i*n*(*g*)koo-men'duzh

English.	Portuguese.	Pronunciation.
postage paid	*franqueado*	frun(*g*)ki-ah'doo [ye(r)
a postage stamp	*uma estampilha*	oom'e(r) ishtum-peel'-
postal (pillar-) box	*caixa pilar postal*	ki'she(r) peelahr' poosh- tahl' [tahl'
a post-card	*um cartão postal*	oon(*g*) kurrtown(*g*)' poosh-
poste-restante	*poste restante*	pawsh'ti reshtun'ti
the postman	*o carteiro*	oo kurrtay'roo
postmaster	*director* (m.) *do cor-*	diraytohr' doo koorray'oo
the post-office	*o correio* [*reio*	oo koorray'oo [men'ti
re-address, to	*endereçar novamente*	indirissahr' nawve(r)-
register (a letter), to	*registar uma carta*	rizh-ishtahr' oom'e(r) kahr'te(r) [ghe(r)
reply paid	*resposta paga*	rishpawsh'te(r) pah'-
a telegraph form	*uma forma para telegramma*	oom'e(r) fohr'me(r) pur'- re(r) tilligrum'me(r)
— — messenger	*um mensageiro de telegrammas*	oon(*g*) mense(r)zhay'roo di tilligrum'muzh
— — office	*escriptorio do telegrapho*	ishkreetaw'rioo doo ti- leg're(r)foo
value of contents	*valor do contheúdo*	ve(r)lohr' doo kohntioo'-
the weight	*o peso*	oo pez'oo [doo
weight, over	*o peso a mais*	— — e(r) mi'zh
—, under	*o peso a menos*	— — e(r) men'oozh

82. Cardinal Numbers. (*Numeros Cardinaes.*)

(For Grammatical Notes see p. 79.)

Portuguese.	Pronunciation.	Portuguese.	Pronunciation.
1 *um* m.,	oon(*g*),	11 *onze*	ohn(*g*)'zi
uma f.	oom'e(r)	12 *doze*	doh'zi
2 *dois* m.,	doy'zh,	13 *treze*	treh'zi
duas f.	doo'uzh	14 *quatorze*	ke(r)tawr'zi
3 *tres*	trezh	15 *quinze*	keen(*g*)'zi
4 *quatro*	kwah'troo	16 *dezaseis*	diz-e(r)say'zh
5 *cinco*	seen(*g*)'koo	17 *dezasete*	diz-e(r)set'i
6 *seis*	saizh	18 *dezoito*	diz-oy'too
7 *sete*	set'i	19 *dezanove*	diz-e(r)naw'vi
8 *oito*	oy'too	20 *vinte*	veen'ti
9 *nove*	naw'vi	21 *vinte e um* (*uma*)	veen'ti oon(*g*), oom'e(r)
10 *dez*	dezh		

	Portuguese.	Pronunciation.
22	*vinte e dois (duas)*	veen'ti doy'zh, doo'uzh
23	— *e tres*	— trezh
24	— *e quatro*	— kwah'troo
25	— *e cinco*	— seen(*g*)'koo
26	— *e seis*	— sayzh
27	— *e sete*	— set'i
28	— *e oito*	— oy'too
29	— *e nove*	— naw'vi
30	*trinta*	treen'te(r)
31	— *e um (uma)*	— i oo*n*(*g*) [oom'e(r)]
40	*quarenta*	kwurren'te(r)
41	— *e um (uma)*	— i oo*n*(*g*) [oom'e(r)]
50	*cincoenta*	see*n*(*g*)koo-en'te(r)
60	*sessenta*	sessen'te(r)
70	*setenta*	set-en'te(r)
80	*oitenta*	oyten'te(r)
90	*noventa*	nooven'te(r)
100	*cem*	say*n*(*g*)
101	*cento e um (uma)*	sent'oo i oo*n*(*g*) [oom'e(r)]
110	— *e dez*	— i dezh
120	— *e vinte*	— i veen'ti
130	— *e trinta*	— i treen'te(r)
200	*duzentos, duzentas*	doozen'toozh, doozen'tuzh
300	*trezentos (as)*	triz-en'toozh (uzh)
400	*quatrocentos (as)*	kwahtroosen'toozh (uzh)
500	*quinhentos (as)*	keen-yen'toozh (uzh)
600	*seiscentos (as)*	sayzh-sen'toozh (uzh)
700	*setecientos (as)*	settisen'toozh (uzh)
800	*oitocentos (as)*	oytoosen'toozh (uzh)
900	*novocentos (as)*	nawvisen'toozh (uzh)
1,000	*mil*	meel
2,000	*dois (duas) mil*	doyzh (doo'uzh) meel
3,000	*tres mil*	trezh meel
10,000	*dez mil*	dezh meel
20,000	*vinte mil*	veen'ti meel
million	*milhão*	meel-yow*n*(*g*)'

1904. One thousand nine hundred and four. (**Nineteen** hundred and four.)

Mil novecentos e quatro.

Meel nawvisen'toozh i kwah'troo.

33. Ordinal Numbers. *(Numeros Ordinaes.)*

English.	Portuguese.	Pronunciation.
The 1st	*o primeiro*	oo preemay'roo
– 2nd	*o segundo*	oo sigoon'doo
– 3rd	*o terceiro*	oo terrsay'roo
– 4th	*o quarto*	oo kwahr'too
– 5th	*o quinto*	oo keen'too
– 6th	*o sexto*	oo sesh'too
– 7th	*o setimo*	oo set'imoo
– 8th	*o oitavo*	oo oytah'voo
– 9th	*o nono*	oo noh'noo
– 10th	*o decimo*	oo dess'imoo
– 11th	*o undecimo*	oo oondess'imoo
– 12th	*o duodecimo*	oo doo-oodess'imoo
– 13th	*o decimo-terceiro*	oo dess'imoo-terrsay'roo
– 14th	*o decimo-quarto*	oo dess'imoo-kwahr'too
– 15th	*o decimo-quinto*	oo dess'imoo-keen'too
– 16th	*o decimo-sexto*	oo dess'imoo-sesh'too
– 17th	*o decimo-setimo*	oo dess'imoo-set'imoo
– 18th	*o decimo-oitavo*	oo dess'imoo-oytah'voo
– 19th	*o decimo-nono*	oo dess'imoo-noh'noo
– 20th	*o vigesimo*	oo vee-zhess'imoo
– 21st	*o vigesimo primeiro*	oo vee-zhess'imoo preemay'roo
– 30th	*o trigesimo*	oo tree-zhess'imoo
– 40th	*o quadragesimo*	oo kwahdre(r)zhess'imoo
– 50th	*o quinquagesimo*	oo keen(*g*)kwe(r)zhess'imoo
– 60th	*o sexagesimo*	oo sexe(r)zhess'imoo
– 70th	*o septuagesimo*	oo septooe(r)zhess'imoo
– 80th	*o octogesimo*	oo oktoo-zhess'imoo
– 90th	*o nonagesimo*	oo nohne(r)zhess'imoo
– 100th	*o centessimo*	oo sentess'imoo
– 1,000th	*o millessimo*	oo milless'imoo
– last	*o ultimo*	oo ool'timoo

34. Collective and Fractional Numbers, &c.
(Numeros Fraccionarios, Collectivos &c.)

All	*todos* m.pl., *todas* [f.pl.	toh'doozh, toh'duzh
a century	*um seculo*	oon(*g*) sek'ooloo
half-a-century	*meio seculo*	may'oo sek'ooloo
a couple (pair)	*um par*	oon(*g*) pahr
double (twice)	*duplo* m., *dupla* f.	doo'ploo, doo'ple(r)

English.	Portuguese.	Pronunciation.
a dozen	*uma duzia*	oom'e(r) doo'zie(r)
half-a-dozen	*meia duzia*	may'e(r) doo'zie(r)
an eighth	*um oitavo*	oo*n*(*g*) oytah'voo
the first time	*a primeira vez*	e(r) primay're(r) vezh
a fourth	*um quarto*	oo*n*(*g*) kwahr'too
a gross	*uma groza* (*grosa*)	oom'e(r) graw'ze(r)
the half	*a metade*	e(r) mitah'di
once	*uma vez*	oom'e(r) vezh
one sort	*uma qualidade*	oom'e(r) kwahleedah'di
a part (portion)	*uma parte*	oom'e(r) pahr'ti
a quarter (¼)	*um quarto*	oo*n*(*g*) kwahr'too
a score	*uma vintena*	oom'e(r) veenten'e(r)
the second time	*a segunda vez*	e(r) sigoon'de(r) vezh
single	*simples*	seem'plizh
a third	*um terço*	oo(*n*)*g* tair'soo
the third time	*a terceiro vez*	e(r) terrsay're(r) vezh
three-fold	*triplicado*	triplikah'doo
three-quarters (¾)	*tres quartos*	trezh kwahr'toozh
twice	*duas vezes*	doo'uzh vez'ezh
the whole, all the	*o todo*	oo toh'doo

35. Adjectives.* (*Adjectivos.*)

The Adjectives in this list which end in o are masculine; they change the o to *a*—those in *ão* merely *drop* the *o*—for the feminine. All the rest are both masculine and feminine. (See p. 79.)

Able, un-	*capaz, in—*	ke(r)pahzh', i*n*(*g*)—
active, in-	*activo, in—*	ahtee'voo, in—
afraid	*medroso*	midroh'zoo
agreeable, dis-	*agradavel, des—*	e(r)gre(r)dah'vel, diz—
angry	*zangado*	zu*n*(*g*)-ghah'doo
anxious	*ancioso*	u*n*(*g*)si-oh'zoo
awkward	*sem geito, desairoso*	say*n*(*g*) zhay'too, diz-i-roh'zoo
bad	*mao*	mow (*like* how)
beautiful	*formoso*	foormoh'zoo
bitter	*amargo*	e(r)mahr'goo
blind	*cego*	seg'oo
bold	*atrevido*	e(r)trivee'doo
brave	*bravo*	brah'voo
bright	*luzente*	loozen'ti

* Some Nouns of quality are included for convenient reference.

English.	Portuguese.	Pronunciation.
breadth, the	*a largura*	e(r) lahrgoo're(r)
broad	*largo*	lahr'goo
busy	*occupado*	ohkoopah'doo
calm	*sereno*	si-ren'oo
careful	*cuidadoso*	kooide(r)doh'zoo
careless	*descuidado*	dishkooidah'doo
certain, un-	*certo, in—*	sair'too, in(*g*)—
cheap	*barato*	be(r)rah'too
cheerful	*alegre*	ul-eg'ri
civil, un-	*cortez, des—*	koortezh', dish—
clean	*limpo*	leem'poo
clear	*claro*	klah'roo
clever	*habil*	ah'bil
cold	*frio*	free'oo
comfortable, un-	*confortavel, não —*	koh*n*(*g*)foortah'vel, [now*ng* —
common, un-	*commum, pouco —*	kohmoo*n*(*g*)', poh'koo —
complete, in-	*completo, in—*	kohmplet'oo, i*n*(*g*)—
continual	*continuo*	kohntee'noo-oh
cool	*fresco*	fresh'koo
correct, in-	*correcto, in—*	koorret'oo, i*n*(*g*)—
cruel	*cruel*	krooel'
curious	*curioso*	kooriooh'zoo
damp	*humido*	oo'midoo
dangerous	*perigoso*	perigoh'zoo
dark	*escuro*	ishkoo'roo
dead	*morto*	mohr'too
deaf	*surdo*	soor'doo
different	*differente*	diffi-ren'ti
dirty	*sujo*	soo'zhoo
distinct	*distincto*	dishteen'too
dry	*secco*	sek'oo
dull	*estupido*	ishtoo'pidoo
dumb	*mudo*	moo'doo
dusty	*empoado*	impooah'doo
eager	*avido*	ah'vidoo
early	*cedo*	seh'doo
easy (not difficult)	*facil, á vontade*	fah'sil, ah vohntah'di
easy (comfortable)	*commodo*	kaw'moodoo
empty	*vazio*	ve(r)zee'oo
every	*cada, todo*	kud'e(r), toh'doo

English.	Portuguese.	Pronunciation.
false (untrue)	*falso*	fahl'soo
famous	*famoso*	fe(r)moh'zoo
fashionable, un-	*em moda, fora da moda*	ain(*g*) maw'de(r), faw'-re(r) de(r) maw'de(r)
fast	*adiantado*	e(r)diuntah'doo
fat (stout)	*gordo*	gohr'doo
favourable, un-	*favoravel, des—*	fe(r)voorah'vel, dish—
few	*poucos*	poh'koozh
fine	*fino*	fee'noo
firm	*firme*	feer'mi
flat	*chato*	shah'too
foolish	*imprudente*	improoden'ti
fortunate, un-	*afortunado, des—*	e(r)foortoonah'doo, diz—
free	*livre*	leev'ri
fresh	*fresco*	fresh'koo
full	*cheio*	shay'oo
general	*geral*	zhurrahl'
generous	*generoso*	zheneroh'zoo
gentle	*meigo*	may'goo
glad	*contente*	kohnten'ti
good	*bom*	bohn(*g*)
grand	*grande*	grun'di
great	*illustre*	illoosh'tri
happy, un-	*feliz, in—*	fileezh', in(*g*)—
hard	*duro*	doo'roo
heavy	*pesado*	pezah'doo
high	*alto*	ahl'too
hilly	*montanhoso*	mohntun-yoh'zoo
hollow	*ouco*	oh'koo
honest, dis-	*honesto, des—*	ohnesh'too, diz—
hot	*quente*	ken'ti
idle	*preguiçoso*	pri-ghissoh'zoo
immediate	*immediato*	immidiah'too
important, un-	*importante, pouco importante*	impoortun'ti, poh'koo impoortun'ti
injurious, un-	*nocivo, innocuo*	noosee'voo, innaw'koo-oo
interesting, un-	*interessante, des—*	interressun'ti, diz—
just, un-	*justo, in—*	zhoosh'too, in(*g*)—
kind, un-	*benigno, pouco amavel*	bineeg'noo, poh'koo e(r)mah'vel

English.	Portuguese.	Pronunciation.
large	*grande*	grun'di
late	*tarde*	tahr'di
length, the	*o comprimento*	oo kohmprimen'too
light (weight)	*ligeiro*	li-zhay'roo
little	*pequeno*	piken'oo
long	*comprido*	kohmpree'doo
loose	*solto*	sohl'too
loud	*estrondoso*	ishtrohndoh'zoo
low	*baixo*	bi'shoo
many	*muitos* m.pl.	moo'intoozh
mild	*brando*	brun'doo
miserable	*miseravel*	meezerrah'vel
modern	*moderno*	moodair'noo
nasty	*sordido*	sohr'didoo
natural, un-	*natural, des—*	ne(r)toorahl', dizh—
necessary, un-	*necessario, des—*	nessessah'rioo, dizh—
nice	*delicado*	dileekah'doo
noble, ig-	*nobre, ignobil*	naw'bri, ignaw'bil
numerous	*numeroso*	noomerroh'zoo
old	*velho*	vel'yoo
open	*aberto*	e(r)bair'too
ordinary, extra-	*ordinario, extra—*	awrdinah'rioo, ish-[tre(r)—
pale	*pallido*	pahl'lidoo
patient, im-	*paciente, im—*	pe(r)sien'ti, im—
perfect, im-	*perfeito, im—*	perrfay'too, im—
plain	*simples*	seem'plizh
pleasant, un-	*aprazivel*	e(r)pre(r)zee'vel
poisonous	*venenoso*	ven-in-oh'zoo
possible, im-	*possivel, im—*	poossee'vel, im—
practical	*practico*	prah'tikoo
present	*presente*	priz-en'ti
pretty	*bonito*	boonee'too
principal	*principal*	prin(g)sipahl'
probable, im-	*provavel, im—*	proovah'vel, im—
quick	*veloz*	vel-awzh'
queer	*exquisito*	ishkizee'too
rare	*raro*	rah'roo
rather	*antes, um pouco*	un'tizh, oon(g) poh'koo
raw	*cru*	kroo
ready	*prompto*	prohn'too

English.	Portuguese.	Pronunciation.
real, un-	*real, illusorio*	riahl', eeloozaw'rioo
reasonable, un-	*razoavel, desara-*	re(r)zooah'vel, dizurre(r)-
regular, ir-	*regular, ir— [zoado*	rigoolahr', ir—[zooah'doo
reliable, un-	*fidedigno*	feedideeg'noo
remarkable	*notavel*	nootah'vel
right	*bem*	bai*n*(*g*)
rude	*rude*	roo'di
rural	*rural*	roorahl'
sad	*triste*	treesh'ti
same	*mesmo*	mezh'moo [now*n*(*g*) —
satisfactory, un-	*satisfactorio, não —*	sutizhfut-aw'rioo,
safe, un-	*salvo, não —*	sahl'voo, now*n*(*g*) —
savage	*selvagem, feroz*	silvi'zhe*n*(*g*), fi-rawzh'
secure, in-	*seguro, não —*	sigoo'roo, now*n*(*g*) —
serious	*serio*	sair'ioo
severe	*severo*	sivair'oo
sick, -ly	*curto*	koor'too
short	*doente, doentio*	dooen'ti, dooentee'oo
silent	*silencioso*	seele*n*(*g*)sioh'zoo
simple	*simples*	seem'plizh
single	*singelo*	see*n*(*g*)-zhel'loo
slight	*leve*	lev'i
slow	*vagaroso*	ve(r)gurroh'zoo
small	*pequeno*	pik-en'oo
smooth	*liso*	lee'zoo
soft	*macio*	mussee'oo
solid	*solido*	saw'lidoo
stormy	*tempestuoso*	tempeshtoo-oh'zoo
straight	*direito*	diray'too
strange	*estranho*	ishtrun'yoo
strong	*forte*	fawr'ti
stupid	*estupido*	ishtoo'pidoo
suitable, un-	*proprio, im—*	praw'prioo, im—
sufficient, in-	*sufficiente, in—*	soofissien'ti, i*n*(*g*)—
sure	*certamente*	sairte(r)men'ti
sweet	*dôce*	doh'si
swift	*rapido*	rah'pidoo
tall	*alto*	ahl'too
terrible	*terrivel*	terree'vel
thick	*grosso, espesso*	grohs'soo, ishpes'soo

English.	Portuguese.	Pronunciation.
thickness, the	*a grossura*	e(r) groossoo're(r)
thin	*delgado, magro*	delgah'doo, mah'groo
thirsty	*sedento*	sed-en'too
tight	*apertado*	e(r)perrtah'doo
timely	*opportuno*	ohppoortoo'noo
tiresome	*enfadonho*	i*n*(*g*)fe(r)dohn'yoo
total	*total*	tootahl'
tough	*duro*	doo'roo
troublesome	*enfadonho*	i*n*(*g*)fe(r)dohn'yoo
true	*verdadeiro*	verrde(r)day'roo
ugly	*feio*	fay'oo
unfit	*incapaz*	i*n*(*g*)ke(r)pahzh'
unsettled	*incerto*	i*n*(*g*)sair'too
usual, un-	*usual, des—*	oozooahl', diz—
urgent	*urgente*	oorzhen'ti
useful	*util*	oo'til
vain	*vão*	vow*n*(*g*)
valuable, in-	*estimavel, in—*	ishteemah'vel, in—
various	*varios*	vah'rioozh
violent	*violento*	veeoolen'too
visible, in-	*visivel, in—*	vizee'vel, i*n*(*g*)—
warm	*quente*	ken'ti
weak	*fraco*	frah'koo
well	*bem*	bai*n*(*g*)
wet	*molhado*	mool-yah'doo
whole	*todo, completo*	toh'doo, koomplai'too
wholesome, un-	*saudavel, insalubre*	se(r)oodah'vel, i*n*(*g*)sul-
wicked	*malvado*	mahlvah'doo [oo'bri
wide	*largo*	lahr'goo [doo
wild	*feroz, desenfreado*	firawzh', diz-i*n*(*g*)friah'-
willing, un-	*prompto, relutante*	prohn'too, rilooktun'ti
windy	*ventoso*	ventoh'zoo
wise, un-	*sabio, imprudente*	sah'bioo, improoden'ti
wonderful	*maravilhoso*	murre(r)veel-yoh'zoo
wooden	*feito de páo*	fay'too di pow (*like* now)
worthless	*indigno, sem valor*	indeeg'noo, sai*n*(*g*) ve(r)-lohr'
wretched	*triste, desgraçado*	treesh'ti, dizhgrussah'doo
wrong	*mal*	mahl
young	*môço*	moh'soo

36. Verbs. (*Verbos.*)

(For Grammatical Notes see pages 82 to 86.)

English.	Portuguese.	Pronunciation.
To accept	*acceitar*	ussaytahr'
to admire	*admirar*	udmeerahr'
to answer	*responder*	rishpohndehr'
to ask	*pedir, perguntar*	pideer', perrgoontahr'
to awake	*acordar*	e(r)koordahr'
to beat	*bater*	be(r)tehr'
to begin	*começar*	koomi-sahr'
to believe	*crêr*	krehr
to blame	*reprehender*	rip-ri-endehr'
to boil	*ferver*	furrvehr'
to borrow	*pedir emprestado*	pideer' imprishtah'doo
to breakfast	*almoçar*	ahlmoosahr'
to bring	*trazer*	truzzehr'
to build	*edificar*	idifikahr'
to button	*abotoar*	e(r)bootooahr'
to buy	*comprar*	kohmprahr'
to calculate	*calcular*	kahlkoolahr'
to carry	*levar*	livahr'
to chat	*palestrar*	pe(r)lishtrahr'
to cook	*cosinhar*	koozin-yahr'
to compare	*comparar*	kohmpurrahr'
to consent	*consentir*	koh*n*(*g*)senteer'
to continue	*continuar*	kohntinooahr'
to cough	*tossir*	toosseer'
to cover	*cobrir*	koobreer'
to dance	*dançar*	du*n*(*g*)sahr'
to deliver	*entregar*	intrigahr'
to deny	*negar*	nigahr'
to depart	*partir*	purrteer'
to descend	*descer*	dizh-sehr'
to desire	*desejar*	diz-izh-ahr'
to despise	*desprezar*	dishprizahr'
to dine	*jantar*	zhuntahr'
to dispute	*disputar*	dishpootahr'
to do	*fazer*	fe(r)zehr'
to doubt	*duvidar*	doovidahr'
to draw (pull)	*puxar*	pooshahr'
to dream	*sonhar*	soon-yahr'

English.	Portuguese.	Pronunciation.
to dress	*vestir*	vishteer'
to drink	*beber*	bibehr'
to excuse	*desculpar*	dishkoolpahr'
to explain	*explicar*	ishplikahr'
to fall	*cahir*	ke(r)-eer'
to feel	*sentir*	senteer'
to find	*achar*	e(r)shahr'
to finish	*acabar*	e(r)ke(r)bahr'
to flatter	*lisongear*	leezohn(g)-zhi-ahr'
to follow	*seguir*	si-gheer'
to forget	*esquecer*	ishkessehr'
to gather	*colher*	kool-yehr'
to get	*obter*	ohbtehr'
to give	*dar*	dahr
to go	*ir*	eer
to go in	*entrar*	intrahr'
to go out	*sahir*	se(r)-eer'
to grow	*crescer*	krizh-sehr'
to hate	*odiar*	ohdiahr'
to hear	*ouvir*	ohveer'
to hide	*esconder*	ishkohndehr'
to hire	*alugar*	e(r)loogahr'
to honour	*honrar*	on(g)rahr'
to hope	*esperar*	ishperrahr'
to be hungry	*ter fome*	tehr faw'mi
to be ignorant of	*ignorar*	eegnoorahr'
to imagine	*imaginar*	ime(r)zhinahr'
to imitate	*imitar*	imitahr'
to insult	*insultar*	in(g)sooltahr'
to insure	*segurar*	sigoorahr'
to introduce	*introduzir*	introodoozeer'
to joke	*zombar*	zohmbahr'
to jump	*saltar*	sahltahr'
to know (a person)	*conhecer*	koon-yissehr'
— — (a thing)	*saber*	sub-ehr'
to land	*desembarcar*	diz-imburrkahr'
to laugh	*rir*	reer
to learn	*aprender*	up-rendehr'
to lend	*emprestar*	imprishtahr'
to lie down	*deitar-se*	daytahr'-si

English.	Portuguese.	Pronunciation.
to live	*viver*	veevehr'
— — (dwell)	*morar*	moorahr'
to look for	*procurar*	prookoorahr'
to lose	*perder*	perrdehr'
to love	*amar*	um-ahr'
to marry	*casar*	kuz-ahr'
to be mistaken	*enganar-se*	*in(g)*gun-ahr'si
to object	*objectar*	ohb-zhet-ahr'
to offend	*offender*	ohffendehr'
to offer	*offerecer*	ohfferressehr'
to open	*abrir*	ub-reer'
to order	*ordenar*	ohrdenahr'
to pack up	*emballar*	imbe(r)l-lahr'
to paint	*pintar*	peentahr'
to pardon	*perdoar*	perrdooahr'
to pay	*pagar*	pe(r)gahr'
to plant	*plantar*	pluntahr'
to play	*jogar*	zhoogahr'
to pluck	*arrancar*	urrunkahr'
to praise	*louvar*	lohvahr'
to present	*apresentar*	up-riz-entahr'
to prove	*provar*	proovahr'
to punish	*castigar*	kushtigahr'
to put on	*pôr*	pohr
to quarrel	*contender*	kohntendehr'
to be quiet	*estar quieto*	ishtahr' ki-et'oo
to read	*ler*	lehr
to reap	*ceifar*	sayfahr'
to reflect	*reflectir*	riflet-eer'
to refuse	*recusar*	rikoozahr'
to regret	*ter pezar*	tehr pizahr'
to rejoice	*regozijar-se*	rigoozizhar'-si
to remember	*lembrar-se*	lembrahr-si
to repay	*retribuir*	ritribooeer'
to repeat	*repetir*	ripiteer'
to repent	*arrepender-se*	urripendehr'-si
to reply	*replicar*	ripleekahr'
to sail	*navegar*	ne(r)vigahr'
to seal	*sellar*	sellahr'
to search	*pesquizar*	pishkeezahr'

English.	Portuguese.	Pronunciation.
to see	*ver*	vehr
to sell	*vender*	vendehr'
to serve	*servir*	serrveer'
to show	*mostrar*	mooshtrahr'
to sigh	*suspirar*	sooshpeerahr'
to sign	*assignar*	ussinnahr'
to sit down	*assentar-se*	ussentahr'-si
to sleep	*dormir*	doo'r-meer'
to sneeze	*espirrar*	ishpirrahr'
to sow	*semear*	simmi-ahr'
to speak	*fallar*	fe(r)lahr'
to spin	*fiar*	feeahr'
to spoil	*estragar*	ishtre(r)gahr'
to steal	*furtar*	foorrtahr'
to stitch	*pespontear*	pishpohnti-ahr'
to study	*estudar*	ishtoodahr'
to swear	*jurar*	zhoorahr'
to take	*tomar*	toomahr'
to take off	*tirar*	teerahr'
to taste	*provar*	proovahr'
to tell	*dizer*	dizehr'
to thank	*agradecer*	e(r)gre(r)disehr'
to think	*pensar*	pe*n*(*g*)sahr'
to be thirsty	*ter sede*	tehr seh'di
to throw	*atirar*	e(r)teerahr'
to touch	*tocar*	tookahr'
to translate	*traduzir*	tre(r)doozeer'
to travel	*viajar*	vee-e(r)-zhahr'
to unbutton	*desabotoar*	diz-e(r)bootooahr'
to uncover	*descobrir*	dishkoobreer'
to unpack	*desenfarda.*	diz-i*n*(*g*)furrdahr'
to wash	*lavar*	le(r)vahr'
to weep, cry	*chorar*	shoorahr'
to weigh	*pesar*	pizahr'
to wish, to will	*desejar*, *querer*	dizizhahr', ki-rehr'
to want	*carecer*	kurrisehr'
to work	*trabalhar*	tre(r)be(r)l-yahr'
to worship	*adorar*	e(r)doorahr'
to wrap	*embrulhar*	imbrool-yahr'
to write	*escrever*	ishkrivehr'

37. Adverbs, Conjunctions, and Prepositions.

(Adverbios, Conjuncções e Preposições.)

(For Grammatical Notes see p. 86.)

English.	Portuguese.	Pronunciation.
About	*cerca de*	sehr'ke(r) di
above	*em cima*	ain(g) see'me(r)
above all	*acima de todos*	ussee'me(r) di toh'doozh
according to	*conforme*	kohn(g)fawr'mi
after, afterwards	*depois*	dipoyzh'
again	*outra vez*	oh'tre(r) vezh
against	*contra*	kohn'tre(r)
all at once	*de repente*	di ripen'ti
almost	*quasi*	kwah'zi
already	*já*	zhah
also	*tambem*	tumbain(g)'
although	*ainda que*	e(r)-een'de(r) ki
altogether	*totalmente*	tootahlmen'ti
always	*sempre*	sem'pri
among	*entre*	en'tri
and	*e*	ee
anywhere	*em qualquer parte*	ain(g) kwahl'kair pahr'ti
around, round	*em roda*	ain(g) raw'de(r)
as [(about)	*como*	koh'moo
as many	*tantos*	tun'toozh
as much	*tanto*	tun'too
as soon as	*logo que*	law'goo ki
at	*á, em*	ah, ain(g)
at first	*ao principio*	ah'oo preen(g)see'pioo
at last	*afinal*	e(r)feenahl'
at least	*pelo menos*	pel'oo men'oozh
at once	*já*	zhah
at present	*presentemente*	prizentimen'ti
badly	*mal*	mahl
because	*porque*	poorr'ki
before	*antes*	un'tizh
behind	*detraz*	ditrah'zh
below (*adv.*)	*em baixo*	ain(g) bi'shoo
below (*prep.*)	*debaixo*	dibi'shoo
besides	*alem d'isso*	e(r)lain(g) dees'soo
better	*melhor*	mil-yawr'

English.	Portuguese.	Pronunciation.
between	*entre*	en'tri
beyond	*alem*	e(r)lai*n*(*g*)'
but	*porém, mas*	poorai*n*(*g*)', muzh
by	*por, com*	poor, koo*n*(*g*)
certainly, surely	*certamente*	serrte(r)men'ti
consequently	*consequentemente*	koh*n*(*g*)sikwen'timen"ti
down	*abaixo, em baixo*	e(r)bi'shoo, ai*n*(*g*) bi'shoo
during	*durante*	doo-run'ti
early	*cedo*	seh'doo
either (*pron.*)	*qualquer dos dois*	kwahl'kair doozh doyzh
either ... or	*ou...ou*	oh...oh
elsewhere	*em qualquer outra* [*parte*	ai*n*(*g*) kwahlkair oh'tre(r) [pahr'ti
enough	*bastante*	be(r)shtun'ti
even if	*ainda quando*	e(r)een'de(r) kwun'doo
everywhere	*em toda a parte*	ai*n*(*g*) toh'de(r) e(r) [pahr'ti
except (*prep.*)	*excepto*	izhsep'too
except that	*salvo que*	sahl'voo ki
far	*longe*	lohn'zhi
further	*mais longe*	mi'zh lohn'zhi
for (*prep.*)	*por, para*	poor, pur're(r)
for (*conj.*)	*porque*	poorkeh'
from	*de*	di
full of	*cheio de*	shay'oo di
hardly	*apenas, difficilmente*	e(r)pen'uzh, diffee'sil- [men"ti
here	*aqui*	e(r)kee'
herewith	*aqui junto*	e(r)kee' zhoon'too
how	*como, porque*	koh'moo, poorkeh'
however	*com tudo isso*	koo*n*(*g*) too'doo ee'soo
how much?	*quanto?*	kwun'too
if	*se*	si
immediately	*immediatamente*	immiddi-ah'te(r)men"ti
in case that	*caso que*	kah'soo ki
in future	*para o futuro*	pur're(r) oo footoo'roo
in, within	*em, dentro*	ai*n*(*g*), den'troo
indeed	*na verdade*	ne(r) verrdah'di
inside	*dentro de*	den'troo di
instead of	*em lugar de*	ai*n*(*g*) loogahr' di
late	*tarde*	tahr'di
less	*menos*	men'oozh
like	*parecido com*	purrisee'doo koo*n*(*g*)

English.	Portuguese.	Pronunciation.
little (*adj.*)	*pequeno, -a*	pi-ken'oo, -e(r)
little (but little)	*pouco*	poh'koo
many times	*muitas vezes*	moo'intuzh vez'ezh
more	*mais*	mi'zh
much	*muito*	moo'intoo
near	*proximo*	praw'simoo
nearly	*quasi*	kwah'zi
neither (*pron.*)	*nem un, nem outro*	nain(*g*) oon(*g*), nain(*g*) oh'troo
neither ... nor	*nem...nem*	nain(*g*)...nain(*g*)
never	*nunca*	noon(*g*)'ke(r)
next to	*logo em seguida*	law'goo aing si-ghee'de(r)
not	*não*	nown(*g*)
not at all	*de forma alguma*	di fawr'me(r) ahlgoo'me(r)
nothing (*pron.*)	*nada*	nah'de(r)
not yet	*ainda não*	e(r)een'de(r) nown(*g*)
now	*agora*	e(r)gaw're(r)
nowhere	*em parte nenhuma*	ain(*g*) pahr'ti nin-yoo'me(r)
of	*de*	di
of course	*por força*	poor fawr'se(r)
often	*frequentemente*	frikwen'timen"ti
only	*só, sómente*	saw, sawmen'ti
opposite	*fronteiro*	frohntay'roo
or	*ou*	oh
otherwise	*aliás*	e(r)leeazh'
out of, outside	*fora de*	fawr'e(r) di
over	*sobre*	soh'bri
perhaps	*talvez*	tahlvezh'
presently, soon	*brevemente, cedo*	brevvimen'ti, seh'doo
previously	*previamente*	prevvi-e(r)men'ti
quickly	*depressa*	dipres'se(r)
rather	*antes*	un'tizh
same (the) (*adj.*)	*o mesmo*	oo mezh'moo
scarcely	*apenas*	e(r)pen'uzh
seldom	*raramente*	rahre(r)men'ti
since (*prep.*)	*desde que*	dezh'di ki
since (*conj.*)	*desde*	dezh'di
so	*assim*	us-seen(*g*)'
some (*adj.*)	*uns, umas; alguns, algumas*	oon(*g*)zh, oom'uzh; ahlgoon(*g*)'zh, ahlgoom'uzh
something (*pron.*)	*alguma cousa*	ahlgoom'e(r) koh'ze(r)

English.	Portuguese.	Pronunciation.
sometimes	*ás vezes*	ahzh vez'ezh
so much	*tanto*	tun'too
soon	*cedo*	seh'doo
suddenly	*subitamente*	soobite(r)men'ti
that	*que*	ki
that is	*isto é*	eesh'too ay
then	*então*	entown(*g*)'
thence	*d'ali*	de(r)lee'
thenceforth	*desde então*	dezh'di entown(*g*)'
there	*ali*	e(r)lee'
therefore	*portanto*	poorrtun'too
through	*por, por via*	poorr, poorr vee'e(r)
thus	*d'esta sorte*	desh'te(r) sawr'ti
to	*a, para*	e(r), pur're(r)
together	*juntamente*	zhoon'te(r)men"ti
too (conj.)	*tambem*	tumbain(*g*)'
too, too much	*muito, demasiado*	moo'intoo, dime(r)ziah'-doo
towards	*para com, do lado de*	pur're(r) koon(*g*), doo [lah'doo di
under	*debaixo*	dibi'shoo
undoubtedly	*sem duvida*	sain(*g*) doo'vid-e(r)
unless	*a não ser que*	e(r) nown(*g*) sehr ki
until	*até*	e(r)tay'
up, upwards	*em cima, para cima*	ain(*g*) see'me(r), pur're(r) [see'me(r)
up (*prep.*)	*em cima de*	ain(*g*) see'me(r) di
upon	*sobre, em cima*	soh'bri, ain(*g*) see'me(r)
very	*muito*	moo'intoo
well	*bem*	bain(*g*)
when	*quando*	kwun'doo
where?	*onde, aonde?*	ohn'di, e(r)-ohn'di?
whilst	*emquanto*	ain(*g*)kwun'too
why?	*porque?*	poorr'ki?
willingly	*voluntariamente*	vooloontah'rie(r)men"ti
with	*com*	koon(*g*)
with, near	*com, proximo*	koon(*g*), praw'simoo
within (*adv.*)	*dentro de*	den'troo di
without (*prep.*)	*sem*	sain(*g*)
yet (*adv.*)	*ainda, demais, alem d'isso*	e(r)een'de(r), dimi'zh, e(r)lain(*g*)' d'ee'soo
yet (*conj.*)	*comtudo, todavia*	kohn(*g*)too'doo, tohde(r)-[vee'e(r)

ELEMENTARY GRAMMAR.

The Article.

The Article in Portuguese varies according to the number and gender of the noun to which it is attached.

The Definite Article is declined as follows :—

Masc. sing., *o*, the ; pl., *os*. Fem. sing., *a* ; pl., *as*.

Examples :—

Masc., *o cavallo*, the horse ; *os cavallos*, the horses.
Fem., *a rua*, the street ; *as ruas*, the streets.

Combined with the prepositions *de* (of, from), *em* (in), and *a* (to) the article is declined thus :—

do, of (*or* from) the	*dos*	*da*	*das*
no, in the	*nos*	*na*	*nas*
ao, to the	*aos*	*á*	*ás*.

Examples :—

Masculine.

Singular.	Plural.
do homem, of (*or* from) the man	*dos homens*, of (from) the men
no quarto, in the room	*nos quartos*, in the rooms
ao quarto, to the room	*aos quartos*, to the rooms.

Feminine.

da mulher, of (from) the woman	*das mulheres*, of (from) the women
na cosinha, in the kitchen	*nas cosinhas*, in the kitchens
á cosinha, to the kitchen	*ás cosinhas*, to the kitchens.

The Indefinite Article has the following forms :—

Masc. sing., *um*, a (pl., *uns*, some). Fem. sing., *uma* ; pl., *umas*.

The plural form is used as an Indefinite Adjective, as :

um livro, a book ; *uns livros*, some books.
uma casa, a house ; *umas casas*, some houses.

The Noun.

I. The Gender of nouns is largely determined by their meaning. The following are **Masculine** :—

(*a*) Names of all males and the occupations, handicrafts, &c., of men.
(*b*) Of mountains, rivers, and winds.
(*c*) Of countries, towns, villages, &c., not ending in *a*.

Feminine are :—

(*a*) Names of females and the occupations of women.
(*b*) Names of trees and fruits, EXCEPT *limoeiro* (lemon tree) *castanheiro* (chestnut tree), and a few others ; *morango* (strawberry) and *marmelo* (quince), &c.

II. Gender is also denoted by the termination of a noun.

(*a*) Nouns ending in *e*, *i*, *o*, and *u* are mostly **masculine**, as:
dente, tooth; *rei*, king; *filho*, a son; *perú*, turkey.

Exceptions: *fonte* (fountain), *chave* (key), *lei* (law), *filhó* (pan-cake), *nau* (ship), which are *Feminine*, as also the names of virtues, vices, faculties, &c., as:

virtude, virtue; *bondade*, goodness; *velhice*, old age.

(*b*) Nouns ending in Consonants are generally **masculine.**

(*c*) Those terminating in *a*, *ã*, or *ão* are as a rule **feminine**, as:
casa, house; *maçã*, apple; *mão*, hand.

Exceptions (masculine) are: *planeta*, planet; *dogma*, dogma; and other words of Greek derivation; also *pão*, bread; *anão*, dwarf.

Number.

As a general rule, nouns singular ending in Vowels, including *ã*, form the plural by adding **s**, as *dia*, *dias*; *tigre*, *tigres*; *boi*, *bois*; *nabo*, *nabos*; *irmã*, *irmãs*. Those ending in Consonants vary as follows:—

Nouns terminating in **ar**, **er**, **ir**, **or**, and **az**, **ez**, **iz**, **oz**, **uz**, in the singular, form the plural by adding **es**, as *mar*, *mares*; *poder*, *poderes*; *martir*, *martires* or *martyres*; *dôr*, *dôres*; *rapaz*, *rapazes*; *mez*, *mezes*; *perdiz*, *perdizes*; *noz*, *nozes*; *luz*, *luzes*.

Nouns terminating in **al**, **ol**, **ul** form the plural by changing the *l* into **es**, thus: *quintal*, *quintaes*; *álcohol*, *álcohoes*; *azul*, *azues*; except *mal*, pl. *males*, and *consul*, pl. *consules*.

Nouns ending in **el** and **il** (long) change these terminations into **eis**, as *broquel*, *broquéis*; *papel*, *papeis*; *movel*, *moveis*; *fossil*, *fosseis*.

Nouns ending in **il** (sharp) change the *l* into **s**, as *ardil*, *ardis*; *funil*, *funis*.

Final **m** in the singular changes into **ns** in the plural, as *homem*, *homens*; *rim*, *rins*; *som*, *sons*; *atum*, *atuns*.

There is no certain rule for forming the plural of nouns singular ending in *ão*, some changing *ão* to *ães*, as *capitão*, *capitães*; *cão*, *cães*; others to *ões*, as *cidadão*, *cidadões*. This is a matter regulated by euphony, and proficiency can only be acquired by experience.

Note.—It may assist the student to know that words ending in **ion** in English end in *ão* in Portuguese, as *submissão*, submission; *commissão*, commission.

Augmentatives and Diminutives.

Augmentatives are formed by adding one or more syllables to a noun, which thus augment its meaning, either in a favourable or unfavourable sense, as:

homem, man; *homemzarrão*, big, strong man.
casaco, coat; *casacão*, great-coat.
mulher, woman; *mulherona*, woman of big stature.

Diminutives have the contrary effect, and are formed by adding *inho* or *zinho* to nouns of the masculine gender, and *inha* and *zinha* to those of the feminine.

Examples of Diminutives are :—

coitado, poor thing ; *coitadinho*, poor little thing.
irmão, brother ; *irmãozinho*, dear little brother.
cabeça, head ; *cabecinha*, little head.
mão, hand ; *mãozinha*, little hand.

NOTE.—Some words appear by their termination to be augmentatives or diminutives, which are not really so ; as *furão*, a ferret ; *atafona*, a horse-mill ; *moinho*, a mill ; *espinha*, a fish-bone.

The Adjective.

Gender.

Adjectives ending in **o** in the masculine change the *o* into **a** for the feminine, as *novo, nova* ; *mão, má*.

Adjectives terminating in *ão* in the masculine end in *ã* in the feminine, as *são, sã*.

Those ending in *m* or *u* for masculine merely add *a* in the feminine, as *um, uma*, one ; *algum, alguma*, some, &c. ; *cru, crua*, raw. *Bom* (good), however, becomes *boa* in the feminine.

As a rule, those ending in *l* or *ez* are common to both genders, with the following exceptions (chiefly names denoting nationality) : *Hespanhol, Hespanhola* ; *Inglez, Ingleza* ; *Portuguez, Portugueza*, &c.

Degrees of Comparison.

There are three degrees, as in English :—

The POSITIVE, as *nobre*, noble ; *grande*, big or great ; *bello*, beautiful.

The COMPARATIVE is formed by employing *mais*, more, and *menos*, less, with the Positive, as *mais bello*, more beautiful ; *menos bello*, less beautiful.

The comparison can be heightened by using *muito mais* or *muito menos*, much more, much less, as *muito mais bello*, much more beautiful.

The SUPERLATIVE degree is formed : (1) By adding *issimo* or *issima* to the Positive, as *rico*, rich, *riquissimo*, exceedingly rich ; *bello*, handsome, *bellissimo*, most handsome. (2) By using *o* (*a*) *mais* with the Positive, as *o mais bello, a mais bella*, the most fair, the fairest.

Some adjectives have an irregular comparison as in English, as

bom, boa, good ;	*melhór*,	*o melhór*	*pequeno*, little ;	*menór*,	*o menór*
máo, bad ;	*peiór*,	*o peiór*	*alto*, high ;	*superiór*,	*o superiór*
grande, great ;	*maiór*,	*o maiór*	*báixo*, low ;	*inferiór*,	*o inferiór*.

Optimo, bonissimo (very good), *summo* (very high), *maximo* (very great), *doutissimo* (very learned), &c., are SUPERLATIVE ABSOLUTE.

Definite Numeral Adjectives.

All CARDINAL numerals are adjectives of the common gender, **EXCEPT** *um, uma*, one ; *dois, duas*, two ; and *duzentos, trezentos*, &c., which change *os* into *as* for the feminine. *Cento* before a noun masculine or feminine becomes *cem*, as *Cem homens*, a hundred men.

Cento can at times be used as a substantive, as *Um cento de castanhas*, a hundred (of) chestnuts ; also all the cardinal numbers, when preceded by an article or another noun of number, as *O cinco de diamantes*, the five of diamonds ; *um oito*, an eight.

The Pronoun.

Personal Pronouns.

Singular.

Nom.	*eu*,	I	*tu*, thou	*elle*,	he, it	*ella*,	she, it
Gen.	*de mim*,	of me	*de ti*	*d'elle*		*d'ella*	
Dat.	*a mim*,	to me	*a ti*	*a elle*		*a ella*	
Acc.	*a mim*,	me	*a ti*	*a elle*		*a ella*	
Abl.	*de mim*,	from me,	*de ti, por ti*	*d'elle, por elle*		*d'ella, por ella.*	
or	*por mim*,	by me					

Plural.

Nom.	*nós*,	we	*vós*, you, ye	*elles* (m.), they		*ellas* (f.), they	
Gen.	*de nós*,	of us	*de vós*	*d'elles*		*d'ellas*	
Dat.	*a nós*,	to us	*a vós*	*a elles*		*a ellas*	
Acc.	*a nós*,	us	*a vós*	*a elles*		*a ellas*	
Abl.	*de nós*,	from us,	*de vós, por vós*	*d'elles, por elles*		*d'ellas, por ellas.*	
or	*por nós*,	by us					

There being no Neuter gender in Portuguese, "it" is expressed either by the masculine or feminine form, as the case may be.

NOTE.—In *speaking* or *writing*, the Nominative cases are only used (1) for emphasis; (2) where the form of a sentence might be ambiguous without the pronoun; (3) in asking questions, when they generally follow the verb; otherwise they are omitted.

The personal pronouns are compounded with the preposition *com*, thus:

commigo (*com mim*), with me, *comnosco* (*com nós*), with us,
comtigo (*com ti*), with thee, *comvosco* (*com vós*), with you.
comsigo (*com si*), with him, her, them,

Com elle, ella, ellas are also used.

Reflective Pronouns.

The Reflective Pronouns *si* (himself, herself, one's-self) is either masculine or feminine. It has no nominative.

Gen. *de si*, of one's-self, himself, or herself.
Dat. *a si*, to one's-self, &c.
Acc. *a si*, one's-self, &c.
Abl. *de si* or *por si*, from *or* by one's-self, &c.

Mesmo and *mesma* are joined to *si* to indicate the masculine and feminine respectively. They may likewise follow personal pronouns, as *eu mesmo*, myself; *elle mesmo*, himself; *ella mesma*, herself; *vós mesmos*, yourselves; *elles mesmos* (m.), *ellas mesmas* (f.), themselves; *o homem mesmo*, man himself; *a mulher mesma*, woman herself.

Conjunctive Pronouns.

These immediately precede or follow the verb that governs them, and are as follows:—

me, to me
te, to thee
se, to himself, herself
lhe, to him, him; to her, her
nos, to us, us
vos, to you, you
lhes, to them, them.

In the Imperative mood *lhe* must always follow the verb, as *Diga-lhe*, tell him; in other moods it may either precede or follow, as *Elle lhe deu* or *Elle deu-lhe*, he gave him.

Se is sometimes followed by *me*, *lhe*, &c.; as *Offerece-se-me*, it is offered to me; *deu-se-lhe*, it was given to him.

Very often the conjunctive pronouns are joined to a verb, preceded or followed by the verb *haver*, as *Dar-lhe-hei tanto dinheiro*, I will give him so much money.

Possessive Pronouns and Adjectives.

	Masculine.		Feminine.	
	Singular.	Plural.	Singular.	Plural.
My, mine,	*o meu*,	*os meus*	*a minha*,	*as minhas*
thy, thine,	*o teu*,	*os teus*	*a tua*,	*as tuas*
his, her, its, his, hers,	*o seu*,	*os seus*	*a sua*, her *or* its,	*as suas*
our, ours,	*o nosso*,	*os nossos*	*a nossa*,	*as nossas*
your, yours,	*o vosso*,	*os vossos*	*a vossa*,	*as vossas.*

Possessive pronouns are preceded by the definite article, except when used predicatively. Possessive adjectives also take the article, except when addressing persons or referring to relatives. Both must agree in number and gender with the nouns which follow them or to which they refer. Examples: *Os meus livros*, my books; *meu pae*, my father; *aquella casa é minha*, that house is mine.

In polite conversation *os seus*, *as suas*, are used for "your, yours."

There is no pronoun corresponding to the English "its."

In addressing a person the pronoun *you* is usually rendered *Vossa mercê* (your worship), contracted into "V.Mcê." in writing, and pronounced "vossmussay'." It is occasionally necessary to apply the titles *Vossa Senhoria* ("V.Sia.") and *Vossa Excellencia* ("V.Excia.") to persons of high rank. Ladies are also addressed in the latter form. The plurals end in *s*.

"Mr." is represented by *Senhor*, and "Mrs." by *Senhora* or *Madama*, but there is no form corresponding to the English "Miss." The titles *Dom* (lord) and *Dona* (lady) are only used before christian names.

Tu (thou) is used in speaking to servants or intimate friends, and *O Senhor* to strangers in polite society.

Demonstrative Pronouns.

Mas. sing.		Mas. plur.		Fem. sing. & plur.	Neut. sing. & plur.	
este,	this	*estes*,	these	*esta*, *estas*	*isto*,	*estes.*
esse,	that	*esses*,	those	*essa*, *essas*	*isso*,	*esses.*
aquelle,	that	*aquelles*,	those	*aquella*, *aquellas*	*aquillo*,	*aquelles.*

Este, *esta* is applied to a person or thing near the speaker.
Esse, *essa* „ „ „ near the person addressed.
Aquelle, *aquella* „ „ equally distant from both.

NOTE.—The masculine and neuter plurals are the same.

Relative Pronouns.

Sing. *que*, which *or* who; *quem*, whom. No plural.
„ *o* (*a*) *qual*, who, which. Pl. *os* (*as*) *quaes*, the which.
„ *cujo* (*a*), whose, of which. Pl. *cujos* (*as*), whose.

Interrogative Pronouns.

Sing. & Pl. *quem?* who?
Sing. ... *qual?* which? Pl. *quaes?*
Sing. & Pl. *que?* what? which?

Quemquer, which has no plural, signifies "whoever," or any person; and *qualquer* (pl. *quaesquer*) "any one," whether man, woman, or thing.

Indefinite Pronouns.

(*a*) Substantival forms:—

alguem, somebody, someone.
ninguem, nobody, no one.
nada, nothing.
fulano, *sicrano*, or *beltrano*, such a one.
outrem, another.

The above have one termination only for the two genders, EXCEPT *fulano*, which has *fulana* f.

(*b*) Adjectival forms:—

Sing. *cada*, each; *certo*, *-a*, Pl. *certos*, *-as*, certain.

(*c*) Substantival and Adjectival forms:—

Sing.	*um*, *uma*, a, one.	Pl.	*uns*, *umas*, some.
,,	*algum*, *alguma*, some.	,,	*alguns*, *algumas*.
,,	*outro*, *outra*, other.	,,	*outros*, *outras*, others.
,,	*todo*, *toda*, all, every.	,,	*todos*, *todas*.
,,	*tal*, such.	,,	*taes*.
,,	*tal qual*, such as.	,,	*taes quaes*.

Cada um or *cada uma* (no plural) signifies "every one," "each."

The Verb.

Auxiliary Verbs.

It is essential to understand first the nature of the four Auxiliary verbs *Ter* and *Haver* (to have), *Ser* and *Estar* (to be).

Ter is nearly always an active verb, and means in that sense *to hold* or *possess*. *Haver* is a true auxiliary, used only in compound future tenses.

Ser implies the essence of a thing, its quantity, and quality; as *ser rico*, to be rich; *ser alto*, to be tall. *Estar* denotes a transitory or accidental state, as *estar doente*, to be ill; *estar em Londres*, to be in London.

Estar may be used before the imperfect participle (gerund), but not *Ser*, as *estou escrevendo*, I am writing.

CONJUGATION OF THE AUXILIARY VERBS.

Infinitive.

Ter,	*Haver*,	to have.	*Ser*,	*Estar*,	been.

Imperfect Participle (Gerund).

tendo,	*havendo*,	having.	*sendo*,	*estando*,	being.

Past Participle.

tido,	*havido*,	had.	*sido*,	*estado*,	to be.

Indicative Mood.

Present.

eu tenho,	*hei,*	I have	*sou,*	*estou,*	I am
tu tens,	*has,*	thou hast	*es,*	*estas,*	thou art
elle tem,	*ha,*	he has	*é,*	*está,*	he is
nós temos,	*havemos* or *hemos,*	we have	*somos,*	*estamos,*	we are
vós tendes,	*haveis, heis,*	you have	*sois,*	*estais,*	you are
elles têm,	*hão,*	they have.	*são,*	*estão,*	they are.

Past Imperfect.

eu tinha,	*havia,*	I had	*era,*	*estava,*	I was
tinhas,	*havias,*	thou hadst	*eras,*	*estavas,*	thou wast
tinha,	*havia,*	he had	*era,*	*estava,*	he was
tinhamos,	*haviamos,*	we had	*eramos,*	*estavamos,*	we were
tinheis,	*havieis,*	you had	*ereis,*	*estaveis,*	you were
tinhão,	*havião,*	they had.	*eram,*	*estavam,*	they were.

Past Definite.

eu tive,	*houve,*	I had	*fui,*	*estive,*	I was
tiveste,	*houveste,*	thou hadst	*foste,*	*estiveste,*	thou wast
teve,	*houve,*	he had	*foi,*	*esteve,*	he was
tivemos,	*houvemos,*	we had	*fomos,*	*estivemos,*	we were
tivestes,	*houvestes,*	you had	*fostes,*	*estivestes,*	you were
tiverão,	*houveram,*	they had.	*foram,*	*estiveram,*	they were.

Future.

eu terei,	*haverei,*	I shall (will) have	*serei,*	*estarei,*	I shall (will) be
terás,	*haverás,*	thou wilt have	*serás,*	*estarás,*	thou wilt be
terá,	*haverá,*	he will have	*será,*	*estará,*	he will be
teremos,	*haveremos,*	we shall have	*seremos,*	*estaremos,*	we shall be
tereis,	*havereis,*	you will have	*sereis,*	*estareis,*	you will be
terão,	*haverão,*	they will have.	*serão,*	*estarão,*	they will be.

Conditional, or Secondary Future.

eu teria,	*haveria,*	I should (would) have	*seria,*	*estaria,*	I should (would) be
terias,	*haverias,*	thou wouldst have	*serias,*	*estarias,*	thou wouldst be
teria,	*haveria,*	he would have	*seria,*	*estaria,*	he would be
teriamos,	*haveriamos,*	we should have	*seriamos,*	*estariamos,*	we should be
terieis,	*havereis,*	you would have	*serieis,*	*estarieis,*	you would be
terião,	*haverião,*	they would have.	*serião,*	*estariam,*	they would be.

Imperative Mood.

tem tu,	*hajas tu,*	have (thou)	*sê tu,*	*está tu,*	be (thou)
tenha elle,	*haja elle,*	let him have	*seja elle,*	*esteja elle,*	let him be
tenhâmos nós,	*hajâmos nós,*	let us have	*sejamos,*	*estejamos,*	let us be
tende vós,	*havei vós,*	have (ye)	*sêde,*	*estai,*	be (ye)
tenhão elles,	*hajão elles,*	let them have.	*sejão,*	*estejão,*	let them be.

Subjunctive Mood.

Present.

que	*tenha,*	*haja,*	*that*	I may have	*seja,*	*esteja,*	I may be, &c.
	tenhas,	*hajas,*		thou mayst have	*séjas,*	*estejas,*	
	tenha,	*haja,*		he may have	*seja,*	*esteja,*	
	tenhâmos,	*hajâmos,*		we may have	*sejâmos,*	*estejâmos,*	
	tenhais,	*hajais,*		you may have	*sejais,*	*estejais,*	
	tenhão,	*hajão,*		they may have.	*sejão,*	*estejão.*	

Past Definite. 1st Form.

que	*tivéra,*	*houvéra,*	that I had (should, would, could, might have) &c.	*fôra,*	*estivéra,*	that I were (might be), &c.
	tivéras,	*houvéras,*		*fôras,*	*estivéras,*	
	tivéra,	*houvéra,*		*fôra,*	*estivéra,*	
	tivéramos,	*houvéramos,*		*fôramos,*	*estivéramos,*	
	tivéreis,	*houvéreis,*		*fôreis,*	*estivéreis,*	
	tivérão,	*houvéram,*		*foram,*	*estivérão.*	

Past Definite. Alternative Form.

que	*tivesse,*	*houvesse,*	*fôsse,*	*estivesse,*
	tivesses,	*houvesses,*	*fôsses,*	*estivesses,*
	tivesse,	*houvesse,*	*fôsse,*	*estivesse,*
	tivessemos,	*houvessemos,*	*fôssemos,*	*estivessemos,*
	tivesseis,	*houvesseis,*	*fôsseis,*	*estivesseis,*
	tivessem,	*houvessem,*	*fôssem,*	*estivessem.*

Future Imperfect.

tiver,	(if *or* when) I shall have, &c.	*fôr,*	*estiver,*	(if *or* when) I shall be, &c.
tiveres,		*fôres,*	*estiveres,*	
tiver,		*for,*	*estiver,*	
tivermos,		*formos,*	*estivermos,*	
tiverdes,		*fordes,*	*estiverdes,*	
tiverem,		*forem,*	*estiverem.*	

NOTE.—The verbs may be conjugated with or without the personal pronouns.

The terminations *ão* and *am* in the 3rd person plural are largely alternative. To make a distinction, however, it is usual to reserve the termination *ão* for the future tense, allowing the other tenses to take the alternative *am*.

The form *ha* is used impersonally to express "there is," "there are."

Regular Verbs.

There are three conjugations, whose infinitives terminate in *ar*, *er*, and *ir* respectively; e.g.,

Infinitive Present.

Amar, to love.	*Vender*, to sell.	*Admittir*, to admit.

Imperfect Participle (Gerund).

amando, loving.	*vendendo*, selling.	*admittindo*, admitting.

Perfect Participle.

amado, loved.	*vendido*, sold.	*admittido*, admitted.

Indicative Mood.

Present.

amo,	I love	*vendo*,	I sell, &c.	*admitto*,	I admit, &c.
amas,	thou lovest	*vendes*,		*admittas*,	
ama,	he loves	*vende*,		*admitte*,	
amâmos,	we love	*vendemos*,		*admittimos*,	
amais,	you love	*vendeis*,		*admittis*,	
amão,	they love.	*vendem.*		*admittem.*	

Past Imperfect.

amava,	I was loving,	*vendia*,	I was selling,	*admittia*,	I was admit-
amavas,	&c.	*vendias*,	&c.	*admittias*,	ting, &c.
amava,		*vendia*,		*admittia*,	
amávamos,		*vendiamos*,		*admittiamos*,	
amaveis,		*vendieis*,		*admittieis*,	
amavão.		*vendião.*		*admittião.*	

Past Definite.

amei,	I loved, &c.	*vendi*,	I sold, &c.	*admitti*,	I admitted,
amaste,		*vendêste*,		*admittiste*,	&c.
amou,		*vendeu*,		*admittiu*,	
amâmos,		*vendêmos*,		*admittimos*,	
amastes,		*vendestes*,		*admittistes*,	
amarão.		*vendêrão.*		*admittião.*	

Future Imperfect.

amarei,	I shall	*venderei*,	I shall sell,	*admittirei*,	I shall
amarás,	(*or* will) love,	*venderás*,	&c.	*admittirás*,	admit,
amará,	&c.	*venderá*,		*admittirá*,	&c.
amaremos,		*venderemos*,		*admittiremos*,	
amareis,		*vendereis*,		*admittireis*,	
amarão.		*venderão.*		*admittirão.*	

Conditional Imperfect.

amaria,	I should	*venderia*,	I should sell,	*admittiria*,	I should
amarias,	(*or* would) love,	*venderias*,	&c.	*admittirias*,	admit,
amaria,	&c.	*venderia*,		*admittiria*,	&c.
amariamos,		*venderiamos*,		*admittiriamos*,	
amarieis,		*venderieis*,		*admittirieis*,	
amarião.		*venderião.*		*admittirião.*	

Imperative Mood.

ama tu,	love (thou)	*vende tu*,	sell (thou),	*admitte tu*,	admit
ame elle,	let him love	*venda elle*,	&c.	*admitta elle*,	(thou),
amemos nós,	let us love	*vendâmos nós*,		*admittâmos nós*,	&c.
amei vós,	love (ye)	*vendei vós*,		*admitti vós*,	
amem elles,	let them love.	*vendão elles.*		*admittão elles.*	

Subjunctive Mood.

The terminations of the Subjunctive Mood are as follows:—

Present.	1st conj.	(*Que eu*) *am-e*, *am-es*, *am-e*, *am-êmos*, *am-êis*, *am-em.*
	2nd „	*vend-a*, *vend-as*, *vend-a*, *vend-amos*, *vend-ais*, *vend-ão* [(*vend-am*).
	3rd „	*admitt-a*, *-as*, *-a*, *-amos*, *-ais*, *-ão* (*-am*).

Imperfect. Alternative forms.	1st conj.	*(Que eu) am-ára, -áras, -ára, -áramos, -áreis, -árão (-aram).*
		(Que eu) am-asse, -asses, -asse, -assemos, -asseis, -assem.
	2nd „	*vend-era, -eras, -era, -eramos, -éreis, -erão (-eram).*
		vend-esse, -esses, -esse, -essemos, -esseis, -essem.
	3rd „	*admitt-ira, -iras, -ira, -iramos, -ireis, -irão (iram).*
		admitt-isse, -isses, -isse, -issemos, -isseis, -issem.
Future.	1st conj.	*am-ar, -ares, -ar, -armos, -ardes, -arem.*
	2nd „	*vend-er, -eres, -er, -ermos, -erdes, -erem.*
	3rd „	*admitt-ir, -ires, -ir, -irmos, irdes, irem.*

The following are the **Irregular Verbs** most in use:—

dar, to give,	*trazer*, to bring,	*ouvir*, to hear,
dizer, to say,	*valer*, to be worth,	*pedir*, to ask,
fazer, to do *or* make,	*ver*, to see,	*repetir*, to repeat,
perder, to lose,	*cahir*, to fall,	*sahir*, to go out,
poder, to be able,	*dirigir*, to direct,	*seguir*, to follow,
querer, to be willing,	*dormir*, to sleep,	*servir*, to serve,
saber, to know,	*ir*, to go,	*vir*, to come.

Adverbs.*

Some adverbs are formed from **feminine adjectives**, or from adjectives ending in **e** or **el**, by adding *mente* thereto; as *primeira, primeiramente*, firstly; *constante, constantemente*, constantly; *fiel, fielmente*, faithfully.

Adverbs are classified under: (1) **Time**, as *presentemente*, at present; *agora*, now; *hontem*, yesterday; (2) **Place**, as *onde*, where; *aqui*, here; (3) **Quantity**, as *quanto*, how much; *quantas*, how many; *tanto*, so much.

Adverbs cannot be formed from Ordinal numbers, as in English, but the Portuguese have *primeiramente* (firstly), *secundariamente* (secondly). To express *thirdly, fourthly*, &c., they say *Em terceiro lugar, em quarto lugar*, and so on. Some adverbs require *a* or *de* to be prefixed to them, as *a miudo*, often; *de parte*, aside.

By changing the last letter of an adjective of the superlative degree into *amente* a superlative adverb is obtained, as *doutissimo*, most learned; *doutissimamente*, most learnedly.

Prepositions.*

Prepositions may be divided into Simple, as *a*, to, *de*, from, *em*, in, *contra*, against, &c., and Compound (or *prepositional phrases*), consisting of a substantive or adverb in conjunction with one or two prepositions, as *em casa de*, at, *antes de*, before, *debaixo de*, under. Some prepositions govern the noun following in the genitive, as *em cima da (de a) mesa*, upon the table; others govern the dative, as *quanto áquillo*, according to that; others, again, the accusative, as *detraz da casa*, behind the house.

Conjunctions and Interjections.

Nothing need be said here regarding the Portuguese Conjunctions and Interjections. The Conjunctions will be found in the list on pp. 73 to 76. For exclamations, &c., see pp. 92, 93.

* For Adverbs and Prepositions see the English-Portuguese list on pp. 73 to 76.

CONVERSATIONAL PHRASES AND SENTENCES.

Useful and Necessary Idiomatic Expressions and Phrases.

(Phrases e Expressões Uteis, Necessarias e Idiomaticas.)

English.	Portuguese.	Pronunciation.
If you please	*Se me faz favor*	si mi fahzh fe(r)vohr'
Thank you [to	*Agradeço-lhe*	e(r)gre(r)dess'ool-yi [di
Have the goodness	*Tenha a bondade de*	ten'ye(r) e(r) bohndah'di
Much obliged	*Muito obrigado*	moo'intoo ohbrigah'doo
Yes, sir	*Sim, senhor*	seen(*g*), sin-yawr'
Yes, miss	*Sim, minha senhora*	seen(*g*), meen'ye(r) sin-yawr'e(r)
No, madam	*Não, senhora*	nown(*g*), sin-yawr'e(r)
Allow me	*Permitta-me*	perrmeet'e(r)-mi
Bring me	*Traga-me*	trah'ghe(r)-mi
Excuse me	*Desculpe-me*	dishkool'pi-mi
Give me	*Dê-me*	deh-mi
Send me	*Mande-me*	mun'di-mi
Tell me	*Diga-me*	dee'ghe(r)-mi
Will you tell me?	*Queira dizer-me?*	kay're(r) dizehr'-mi?
Does anyone here speak English?	*Ha aqui alguem que falle Inglez?*	ah e(r)kee' ahlgain(*g*)' ki fahl'li inglezh'?
Can you read Portuguese?	*Pode V. Mcê. ler Portuguez?*	paw'di vossmussay' lehr poortoogezh'?
You read very well	*V. Mcê. lê muito bem*	vossmussay' leh moo'intoo bain(*g*)
Who taught you?	*Quem o ensinou?*	kain(*g*) oo in(*g*)sinoh'?
How long have you learned?	*Ha quanto tempo está V.Mcê. aprendendo?*	ah kwun'too tem'poo ishtah' vossmussay' e(r)prenden'doo?
A short time only	*Pouco tempo somente*	poh'koo tem'poo saw-men'ti
I find the pronunciation difficult	*Acho a pronuncia difficil*	ah'shoo e(r) proonoon(*g*)'-sie(r) diffee'sil
You have a good accent	*V.Mcê. tem boa pronuncia*	vossmussay' tain(*g*) boh'-e(r) proonoon(*g*)'sie(r)

English.	Portuguese.	Pronunciation.
I should like to speak to you	*Desejava fallar-lhe*	diz-i-zhah've(r) fe(r)-lahr'l-yi
What can I do for you?	*Em que posso servir-lhe?*	ain(*g*) ki paw'soo serr-veer'l-yi?
You are too kind	*V. Mcê. faz-me muito favor*	vossmussay' fahzh-mi moo'intoo fe(r)vohr'
I am deeply grateful to you	*Fico-lhe summamente grato*	fee'kool-yi soome(r)men'-ti grah'too
Please take a seat	*Queira sentar-se*	kay're(r) sentahr'-si
What do you want?	*Que quer V.Mcê.?*	ki kair vossmussay'?
What do you mean?	*Que quer V.Mcê. dizer?*	ki kair vossmussay' diz-ehr'?
At your service	*Fico ao seu serviço*	fee'koh ah'oo seh'oo serrvee'soo
I believe (think) so	*Creio (julgo) que sim*	kray'oo (zhool'goo) ki seen(*g*)
I believe (think) not	*Creio (julgo) que não*	kray'oo (zhool'goo) ki nown(*g*)
What do you say?	*Que diz V.Mcê?*	ki deezh vossmussay?
I have nothing to say against it	*Nada tenho que dizer contra isso*	nah'de(r) ten'yoo ki dee-zehr' kohn'tre(r) ee'soo
I beg your pardon	*Peço-lhe perdão*	pessool'yi perrdown(*g*)'
What did you ask?	*Que perguntou V.Mcê.?*	ki perrgoontoh' voss-mussay'?
Speak louder	*Falle mais alto*	fahl'li mi'z ahl'too
What does it signify?	*O que quer dizer isto?*	oo ki kair dizehr' eesh'-too?
It does not matter	*Não importa*	nown(*g*) eempawr'te(r)
It is all the same to me	*Para mim é tudo o mesmo*	pur're(r) meen(*g*) ay too'-doo oo mezh'moo
Never mind	*Não faça caso*	nown(*g*) fah'se(r) kah'zoo
What is the matter?	*Que ha?*	ki ah?
What is it about?	*De que se trata?*	di ki si trah'te(r)?
What is to be done?	*Que se ha de fazer?*	ki si ah di fe(r)zehr'?
I have no idea	*Não faço idêa*	nown(*g*) fah'soo eeday'e(r)
Do you understand?	*Entende V.Mcê.?*	inten'di vossmussay'?
I understand	*Entendo*	inten'doo
I do not understand	*Não entendo*	nown(*g*) inten'doo
Carry this	*Leve isto*	lev'eesh'too
Take this away	*Tire isto*	teer'eesh'too
Make haste!	*De pressa!*	di pres'se(r)!
Come along!	*Venha!*	ven'ye(r)!

English.	Portuguese.	Pronunciation.
Take care!	*Tome cuidado!*	taw'mi kooidah'doo!
Look out!	*Cautella!*	kowtel'le(r)!
Listen!	*Ouça V.Mcê.!*	oh'se(r) vossmussay'!
Come in!	*Entre!*	en'tri!
Come here!	*Venha cá!*	ven'ye(r) kah!
Go away!	*Va se embora!*	vahsi imbaw're(r)!
This way	*Por aqui*	poor e(r)kee'
That way	*Por ali*	poor e(r)lee'
Too soon	*Muito cedo*	moo'intoo seh'doo
Too late	*Muito tarde*	moo'intoo tahr'di
Sooner or later	*Mais tarde, menos tarde*	mi'zh tahr'di, men'oozh tahr'di
Very well	*Muito bem*	moo'intoo bain(*g*)
Not very well	*Não muito bem*	nown(*g*) moo'intoo bain(*g*)
It snows	*Cae neve*	ki nev'i
It freezes	*Gela*	zhel'le(r)
It thaws	*Degela*	di-zhel'le(r)
It is very dirty	*Ha lamaceira.*	ah lummussai're(r)
Is it slippery?	*Escorrega?*	ishkoorreg'e(r)?
I nearly fell	*Quasi cahi*	kwah'zi ke(r)-ee'
Do you think it will rain?	*Crê V.Mcê. que choverá?*	kreh vossmussay' ki shooverrah'?
I am afraid so	*Temo que sim*	tem'oo ki seen(*g*)
It is very windy	*Faz muito vento*	fahzh moo'intoo ven'too
How cold it is!	*Que frio faz!*	ki free'oo fahzh!
It is very cold	*Faz muito frio*	fahzh moo'intoo free'oo
It is very warm	*Faz muito calor*	— — ke(r)lohr'
We must soon begin to have a fire	*Em breve teremos de aquecer a casa*	ain(*g*) brev'i ti-rem'oozh di ukkessehr' e(r) kah'ze(r)
It is dark	*Está escuro*	ishtah' ishkoo'roo
It will soon be dark	*Em breve estará escuro*	ain(*g*) brev'i ishturrah' ishkoo'roo
It is a fine day	*O dia está lindo*	oo dee'e(r) ishtah' leen'doo
In broad day	*Em pleno dia*	ain(*g*) plen'oo dee'e(r)
Of course	*Está visto*	ishtah' veesh'too
On the contrary	*Pelo contrario*	pel'oo kohntrah'rioo
Once for all	*Mais uma vez*	mi'z oom'e(r) vezh
After all	*Afinal*	e(r)feenahl'
The other day	*O outro dia*	oo oh'troo dee'e(r)
At the end of a year	*No fim de um anno*	noo feen(*g*) di oon(*g*) un'noo

English.	Portuguese.	Pronunciation.
Between ourselves	*Entre nós*	en'tri nawzh
Everybody knows it	*Todo o mundo o sabe*	toh'doo oo moon'doo oo sah'bi
That is of no consequence	*É pouca cousa*	ay poh'ke(r) koh'ze(r)
I remember it	*Lembro-me d'isso*	lem'broo-mi d'ee'soo
All at once	*Todo de uma vez*	toh'doo di oom'e(r) vezh
Ever so little	*Por pouco que seja*	poor poh'koo ki seh'zhe(r)
Leave me alone	*Deixe-me ficar só*	daysh'mi fikahr' saw
You are joking	*Está zombando*	ishtah' zohmbun'doo
You are right	*Tem razão*	tai*n*(*g*) ruz-ow*n*(*g*)'
Don't be angry	*Não se zangue*	now*n*(*g*) si zu*n*(*g*)'ghi
That depends	*Isso depende*	ee'soo dipen'di
I give it up	*Rendo-me*	ren'doo-mi
So much the more	*Tanto mais*	tun'too m*i*'zh
For want of time	*Por falta de tempo*	poor fahl'te(r) di tem'poo
With all my heart	*Com todo meu coração*	koh*n*(*g*) toh'doo meh'oo koorussow*n*(*g*)'
Do your best	*Faça o melhor possivel*	fah'se(r) oo mil-yawr' poossee'vel
I am going to town	*Vou á cidade*	voh ah seedah'di
Are you going anywhere?	*Vae V.Mcê. a alguma parte?*	v*i* vossmussay' e(r) ahlgoo'me(r) pahr'ti?
Up stairs	*Arriba; lá em cima*	ur-ree'be(r); lah ai*n*(*g*) see'me(r)
Down stairs	*Abaixo*	e(r)b*i*'shoo'
From top to bottom	*De cima abaixo*	di see'me(r) e(r)b*i*'shoo
I am in a hurry	*Estou com pressa*	ishtoh' koo*n*(*g*) pres'se(r)
I dine out (in town)	*Janto fóra (na cidade)*	zhun'too faw're(r) [ne(r) seedah'di]
Where have you come from?	*De onde vem V.Mcê.?*	di ohn'di vai*n*(*g*) vossmussay' re(r)?
Don't go away	*Não se vá embora*	now*n*(*g*) si vah imbaw're(r)
I shall go home	*Irei a casa*	i-ray' e(r) kah'ze(r)
He has come back	*Elle já voltou*	el'li zhah vawltoh'
On horseback	*A cavallo*	e(r) ke(r)vahl'loo
Neither do I	*Nem eu tampouco*	nai*n*(*g*) eh'oo tu*n*(*g*)poh'koo
Some way or another	*De um ou outro modo*	di oo*n*(*g*) oh oh'troo maw'doo
In the meantime	*No entanto*	noo i*n*(*g*)tun'too
You do it in vain	*V. Mcê. o faz debalde*	vossmussay' oo fahzh dibahl'di

English.	Portuguese.	Pronunciation.
Would you kindly	*Queira ter a bondade*	kay're(r) tehr e(r) bohndah'di [gahr'
First of all	*Em primeiro logar*	ain(g) preemay'roo loo-
That is what vexes me	*Isso é o que me rala*	ee'soo ay oo ki mi rah'le(r)
He has just come in	*Elle acaba de entrar*	el'li e(r)kah'be(r) di entrahr'
He pretends	*Elle finge*	el'li feen(g)'zhi
Don't imagine	*Não imagine*	nown(g) eeme(r)zhee'ni
Within everybody's reach	*Ao alcance de todos*	ah'oo ahlkun(g)'si di toh'doozh
What good is it?	*De que vale isso?*	di ki vahl' ee'soo?
As for me	*Quanto a mim*	kwun'too e(r) meen(g)
In a good temper	*De bom modo*	di bohn(g) maw'doo
From day to day	*De dia a dia*	di dee'e(r) e(r) dee'e(r)
Unknown to me	*Sem eu saber*	sain(g) eh'oo sub-ehr'
At the latest	*O mais tardar*	oo mi'zh turrdahr'
You speak at random	*V. Mcê. falla desatinadmente*	vossmussay' fahl'le(r) dize(r)teenah'de(r)men"ti
I did it in a hurry	*Fi-lo com pressa*	fee'loo koon(g) pres'se(r)
He may say what he likes	*Elle pode dizer o que quizer*	el'li paw'di deezehr' oo ki keezehr' [eh'oo?
Where was I?	*Aonde estava eu?*	e(r)ohn'di ishtah've(r)
He began to laugh	*Elle começou a rir*	el'li koomessoh' e(r) reer
I cannot see any longer	*Já não posso ver mais*	zhah nown(g) paw'soo vehr mi'zh
It only depends upon you	*Isso só depende de V. Mcê.*	ee'soo saw dipen'di di vossmussay'
One is as good as the other	*Tanto vale um como outro*	tun'too vah'li oon(g) koo'moo oh'troo
I can do without it	*Posso dispensar com elle*	paw'soo dishpen(g)sahr' koon(g) el'li
Will you give me?	*Queira dar-me?*	kay're(r) dahr'-mi?
Everything considered	*Tomando tudo em consideração*	toomun'doo too'doo ain(g) kohn(g)seederrussown(g)'
He will do just the same	*Elle fará justamente o mesmo*	el'li furrah' zhooshte(r)-men'ti oo mezh'moo
I am sure of it [you	*Estou certo*	ish-toh' sair'too
I have come to tell	*Vim dizer-lhe*	veen(g) deezehr'l-yi

English.	Portuguese.	Pronunciation.
I don't think much of it	*Faço pouca conta d'elle (d'ella)*	fah'soo poh'ke(r) kohn'-te(r) del'li [del'le(r)]
She is always well dressed	*Ella está sempre bem vestida*	el'le(r) ishtah' sem'pri bain(*g*) vishtee'de(r)
No sooner said than done	*Feito logo que dito*	fay'too law'goo ki dee'too
I can bear it no longer	*Já não o posso aturar*	zhah nown(*g*) oo paw'soo e(r)toorahr'
I like being here	*Gosto de estar aqui*	gawsh'too di ishtahr' e(r)-kee'
I have been told	*Disseram-me*	deessair'un(*g*)-mi
As much as I can	*Tanto quanto posso*	tun'too kwun'too paw'soo
That comes to the same thing	*Isso vem a dar na mesma*	ee'soo vain(*g*) e(r) dahr ne(r) mezh'me(r)
I value it very much	*Muito o aprecio*	moo'intoo oo up-ri-see'oo
I am used to it	*Estou acostumado*	ishtoh' e(r)kooshtoo-mah'doo
I am not able to do it	*Não o posso fazer*	nown(*g*) oo paw'soo fe(r)-zehr'
Who is it calls me?	*Quem é que me chama*	kain(*g*) ay ki mi shum'-e(r)
It is not my fault	*Não é a minha culpa*	nown(*g*) ay e(r) meen'-ye(r) kool'pe(r)
That is just like you	*É V. Mcê. tal e qual*	ay vossmussay' tahl i kwahl
Give him that from me	*Dê-lhe isso de minha parte*	dehl'yi ee'soo di meen'-ye(r) pahr'ti
He is my friend	*É amigo meu*	ay e(r)mee'goo meh'oo
Don't stir	*Não se mexa*	nown(*g*) si mesh'e(r)
Will you have some?	*Quer V. Mcê. algum?*	kair vossmussay' ahl-goon(*g*)'?
Not long ago	*Ha pouco tempo*	ah poh'koo tem'poo
He owes me a grudge	*Elle tem quizilha contra mim*	el'li tain(*g*) keezeel'ye(r) kohn'tre(r) meen(*g*)

Expressions of Surprise, Sorrow, Joy, Anger, &c.

(Expressões de Surpresa, Tristeza, Alegria, Colera, &c.)

What?	*O que?*	oo ki?
Is it possible?	*É possivel?*	ay poossee'vel?
Indeed!	*Na verdade!*	ne(r) verrdah'di!
	Devéras!	divair'uzh!
That is impossible	*Isso é impossivel*	ee'soo ay impossee'vel

English.	Portuguese.	Pronunciation.
That cannot be	*Isso não póde ser*	ee'soo nown(*g*) paw'di sehr
You surprise me	*V. Mcê. surprende-* [*me*	vossmussay' soorpren'di- [mi
Don't touch	*Não toque!*	nown(*g*) taw'ki!
My fault	*Minha culpa*	meen'ye(r) kool'pe(r)
Oh! it's nothing!	*Oh! isso não é nada!*	aw! ee'soo nown(*g*) ay nah'de(r)!
I am sorry for it	*Sinto o muito*	seen'too oo moo'intoo
I am quite vexed about it	*Isso bastante me tem vexado*	ee'soo be(r)shtun'ti mi tain(*g*) veshah'doo
What a pity!	*Que pena!*	ki pen'ne(r)!
It is a sad thing	*É lastimôso*	ay lushteemoh'zoo
I am very glad	*Estou muito contente* [*mim!*	ishtoh' moo'intoo kohnten'ti [meen(*g*)!
How happy I am!	*Que felicidade para*	ki filissidah'di pur're(r)
He is very angry	*Elle está muito zangado*	el'li ishtah' moo'intoo zun(*g*)-gah'doo
He is in a bad temper	*Elle está de máo humor*	el'li ishtah' di mow oomohr'
Hold your tongue	*Cale-se V.Mcê.*	kahl'si vossmussay'
You are very wrong	*V. Mcê. engana-se muito*	vossmussay' in(*g*)-gun'e(r)-si moo'intoo
What a shame!	*Que vergonha!*	ki verrgohn'ye(r)!
How could you do so?	*Como pôde fazer isso?*	koo'moo poh'di fuzzehr' ee'soo?
I am ashamed of you	*Estou envergonhado de si*	ishtoh' in(*g*)verrgoonyah'doo di see
For shame!	*Que vergonha!*	ki verrgohn'ye(r)!
You are very much to blame	*Tem muita culpa*	tain(*g*) moo'inte(r) kool'pe(r)
Don't answer [pose	*Não responda*	nown(*g*) rishpohn'de(r)
It answers the pur-	*Serve para o que é*	sair'vi pur're(r) oo ki ay

Making Enquiries. *(Fazendo Perguntas.)*

Do you hear me?	*Ouve-me V.Mcê.?*	ohv'-mi vossmussay'?
Will you kindly...? [me?	*Queira ter a bondade...?*	kay're(r) tehr e(r) bohndah'di...?
Do you understand	*Comprehende-me?*	kohmpri-en'di-mi?
What is that?	*Que é isso?*	ki ay ee'soo?
Are you sure?	*Está certo?*	ishtah' sair'too?

English.	Portuguese.	Pronunciation.
Where is...?	*Onde está ...?*	ohn'di ishtah'...?
What do you call that?	*Como chama a isso?*	koomoo' shum'e(r) e(r) ee'soo?
What does that mean?	*O que significa isso?*	oo ki signifee'ke(r) ee'-soo?
What is that for?	*Para que é isso?*	purre(r) ki ay ee'soo?
Can I see Mr. H.?	*Posso fallar com o Senhor H.?*	paw'soo fe(r)llahr' koon(g) oo sin-yawr' H.?
When does he re-[turn?	*Quando volta elle?*	kwun'doo vohl'te(r) el'li?
Please give him my card	*Queira dar-lhe o meu bilhete*	kay're(r) dahr'l-yi oo meh'oo beelyet'i
I will call again to-morrow, between 10 and 11 a.m.	*Voltarei ámanhã entre as dez e onze da manhã*	vohlturray' ahmun-yun(g)' en'tri uzh dezh i ohn(g)'zi de(r) mun-yun(g)'

Notices. (*Avizos.*)

English.	Portuguese.	Pronunciation.
Apartments	*Quartos*	kwahr'toozh
Bedroom for single gentleman	*Dormitorio para solteiro*	doo'r-meetaw'rioo pur'-re(r) sawltay'roo
Entrance	*Entrada*	intrah'de(r)
Exit	*Sahida*	se(r)ee'de(r)
Fire alarm	*Signal de incendio*	seenahl' di in(g)sen'dioo
Furnished rooms	*Quartos mobilados*	kwahr'toozh moobilah'-doozh
Just published	*Apenas publicado*	e(r)pen'uzh pooblikah'-[doo
Keep off the grass	*Não pise a herva*	nown(g) pee'zi e(r) air'-[ve(r)
Knock; ring	*Bata; toque*	bah'te(r); taw'ki
Walk in!	*Entre!*	en'tri!
Notice!	*Avizo!*	e(r)vee'zoo!
No admittance	*A entrada é prohibida*	e(r) intrah'de(r) ay proh-ibee'de(r)
No smoking allowed	*É prohibido fumar*	ay proh-ibee'doo foo-mahr'
No thoroughfare	*Não ha caminho*	nown(g) ah ke(r)meen'-[yoo
Please do not touch	*Sirva-se não tocar*	seer've(r)-si nown(g) tookahr'
Please wipe your feet	*Sirva-se limpar os pés*	seer've(r)-si leempahr' oozh payzh
Private	*Particular*	purrteekoolahr'

English.	Portuguese.	Pronunciation.
Public notice!	*Avizo publico!*	e(r)vee'zoo poob'leekoo!
Pull; push	*Puxe; empurre*	poo'shi; impoor'ri
Refreshments	*Refrescos*	rifresh'koozh
To be let	*Aluga-se*	e(r)loo'ghe(r)-si
Unfurnished rooms	*Quartos sem mobilia*	kwahr'toozh sain(g) moobee'lie(r)

The Railway. *(O Caminho de Ferro.)*

(See Vocabulary 23, p. 43.)

English.	Portuguese.	Pronunciation.
To the station	*Para a estação*	pur're(r) e(r) ishtussown(g)'
Here is my luggage	*Aqui está a minha bagagem*	e(r)kee ishtah' e(r) meen'ye(r) be(r)ghi'zhen(g)
Take it to the cloak-room	*Leve-a para o deposito de bagagens*	lev'i-e(r) pur're(r) oo dipaw'zitoo di be(r)ghi'zhen(g)zh
I wish to register my luggage for...	*Desejo registar a minha bagagem para...*	diz-ezh'oo rizh-eeshtahr' e(r) meen'ye(r) be(r)ghi'zhen(g) purre(r)...
The luggage is over weight	*A bagagem pesa de mais*	e(r) be(r)ghi'zhen(g) pez'e(r) di mi'zh
Get my luggage; here is the ticket	*Obtenha a minha bagagem; aqui está o bilhete*	ohbten'ye(r) e(r) meen'ye(r) be(r)ghi'zhen(g); e(r)kee ishtah' oo beelyet'i
Where is the waiting-room?	*Onde é a sala de espera?*	ohn'di ay e(r) sah'le(r) di ishpair'e(r)?
— is the booking-office?	*— se compram os bilhetes?*	— si kohm'prun(g) oozh beelyet'izh?
— is the buffet?	*— é o bufete?*	— ay oo boofet'i?
— is the lavatory?	*— é o lavatorio?*	— ay oo luvve(r)taw'rioo?
— is the train for ...?	*— está o comboio para...?*	— ishtah' oo kohmboy'oo pur're(r) ...?
Are you going by the express?	*Vai pelo expresso?*	vi pel'oo ishpres'soo?
Show me a time-table	*Mostre-me o horario*	mawsh'tri-mi oo awrahr'ioo
When does the train start?	*Quando parte o comboio?*	kwun'doo pahr'ti oo kohmboy'oo?

English.	Portuguese.	Pronunciation.
Can I book through to ... ?	*Posso tomar passagem corrida até... ?*	paw'soo toomahr' pe(r)-si'zhen(g) koorree'-de(r) uttay'... ?
A first (second) class single ticket to...	*Um bilhete simples de primeira (segunda) classe até...* [*volta*	oon(g) beelyet'i seem'-plizh di preemay're(r) [sigoon'de(r)] klahss'i uttay'... [vawl'te(r)
Return tickets	*Bilhetes de ida e*	beel-yet'izh di ee'de(r) i
How much is it ?	*Quanto custa ?*	kwun'too koosh'te(r) ?
We want a sleeping carriage	*Queremos uma carruagem de dormir*	ki-rem'oozh oom'e(r) kurrooi'zhen(g) di doo'r-meer'
A corridor carriage	*Uma carruagem salão* [*ras*	oom'e(r) kurrooi'zhen(g) se(r)lown(g)' [ruzh
A carriage for ladies	— — *para senho-*	— — purre(r) sin-yaw'-
A non-smoking compartment [for ... ?	*Um compartimento onde não se fume* [*para...?*	oon(g) kohmpurrtimen'-too ohn'di nown(g) si foo'mi [purre(r)...?
Is this the train	*É este o comboio*	ay esh'ti oo kohmboy'oo
Do I change anywhere on the journey ?	*Tenho de mudar em alguma parte durante a jornada ?*	ten'yoo di moodahr ain(g) ahlgoom'e(r) pahr'ti doo-run'ti e(r) zhoor-nah'de(r) ?
Where must I change for ... ?	*Para... onde devo mudar ?*	pur're(r)... ohn'di dev'oo moodahr' ?
Is this seat engaged ?	*Está tomado este assento ?*	ishtah' toomah'doo esh'-ti ussent'oo ?
There is no room	*Não ha lugar*	nown(g) ah loogahr'
Call the guard	*Chame o guarda*	shum'i oo gwahr'de(r)
The train is just going to start	*O comboio está prestes a partir*	oo kohmboy'oo ishtah' presh'tiz e(r) purrteer'
Open the door	*Abra a portinhola*	ah'bre(r) e(r) poorteen-yaw'le(r) [se(r)
— the window	*Abaixe a vidraça*	e(r)bi'shi e(r) veedrah'-e(r)
Here is the station	*Aqui está a estação*	e(r)kee' ishtah' e(r) ish-tussown(g)'
Do we stop here ?	*Paramos aqui ?*	purrum'ooz e(r)kee' ?
Do we alight here?	*Apeamo-nos aqui ?*	e(r)pi-um'oo-nooz — ?
Do we change carriages here ?	*Mudamo-nos de carruagens aqui ?*	moodum'oo-noozh di kur-rooi'zhen(g)z e(r)kee'?

English.	Portuguese.	Pronunciation.
How long do we stop here?	*Quanto tempo paramos aqui?*	kwun'too temp'oo purrum'ooz e(r)kee'?
Five minutes	*Cinco minutos*	seen(g)'koo meenoo'toozh
The luggage-train	*O comboio da bagagem*	oo kohmboy'oo de(r) be(r)ghi'zhen(g)
Send this by fast train	*Mande isto por comboio de grande velocidade*	mun'di eesh'too poor kohmboy'oo di grun'di viloosidah'di
By slow train	*Por comboio de pequena velocidade*	poor kohmboy'oo di piken'e(r) viloosidah'di
My luggage is lost	*A minha bagagem perdeu-se*	e(r) meen'ye(r) be(r)ghi'zhen(g) perrdeh'oo-si
If it arrives by next train, forward it on to ...	*Se chegar pelo seguinte comboio, faça-a seguir para ...*	si shigahr' pel'oo sighin'ti kohmboy'oo, fah'se(r)-e(r) si-gheer' pur're(r)
Give me your ticket	*Dê-me o seu bilhete*	deh'-mi oo seh'oo beelyet'i
Here it is	*Eil-o aqui*	ayl'-oo e(r)kee'

The Steamboat. (*O Vapor.*)

(See Vocabularies 22 & 23, pages 42 to 44.)

When do we start?	*Quando partimos?*	kwund'oo purrtee'moozh?
When shall we arrive?	*— chegaremos?*	— shigurrem'oozh?
Time is up!	*Já é tempo!*	zhah eh tem'poo!
Wait for me!	*Espere par mim!*	ishpair'i poor meen(g)!
Where is your luggage?	*Onde está a sua bagagem?*	ohn'di ishtah' e(r) soo'-e(r) be(r)ghi'zhen(g)?
Let us go down into the cabin	*Desçamos á camara*	desh'se(r)moozh ah kum'urre(r)
Where is my berth?	*Qual é o meu beliche?*	kwahl' eh oo meh'oo billee'shi?
I want a cabin to myself	*Quero um camarote para mim só*	kair'oo oon(g) kummuraw'ti pur're(r) meen(g) saw
Look for my things	*Procure as minhas cousas*	prookoo'ri uzh meen'yuzh koh'zuzh
There was another trunk	*Havia outro bahú*	uv-ee'e(r) oh'troo bah-oo'
Come to the Custom-house	*Venha á Alfandega*	ven'ye(r) ah ahlfun'dighe(r)

English.	Portuguese.	Pronunciation.
The Custom-house officer	*O guarda da Alfandega*	oo gwahr'de(r) de(r) ahl-fun'di-ghe(r)
Have you your passport ?	*Tem V.Mcê. o seu passaporte ?*	tain(*g*) vossmussay' oo seh'oo pusse(r)pawr'ti?
Will you examine this trunk ?	*Queira V.Mcê. examinar este bahú?*	kay're(r) vossmussay' iz-um-inahr'esh'ti bah-oo'?
Here are the keys	*Eis aqui as chaves*	aiz e(r)kee' uz shah'vizh
Have you anything to declare ?	*Tem V.Mcê. qualquer cousa sugeito a direitos ?*	tain(*g*) vossmussay' kwahl'kair koh'ze(r) soo-zhay'too e(r) di-ray'toozh ?
I have nothing liable to duty	*Nada tenho sugeito a direitos*	nah'de(r) ten'yoo soo-zhay'too e(r) diray'-toozh
What is the duty ?	*Quanto é o imposto?*	kwun'too ay oo eem-pohsh'too ?
Is my luggage passed ?	*Está despachada a minha bagagem ?*	ishtah' dishpe(r)shah'-de(r) e(r) meen'ye(r) be(r)ghi'zhen(*g*) ?
Can I remove it ?	*Posso removel-a ?*	paw'soo rimoovel'-e(r) ?
Passengers are requested to keep clear of the gangways	*Pede-se aos senhores passageiros que se afastem dos passadiços*	ped'si ah'oozh sinyawr'-izh pus-se(r)zhay'roozh ki si e(r)fahsh'ten(*g*) doozh pus-se(r)dee'soozh

Arrival. *(Chegada.)*

Call a cab	*Chame um trem*	shum'i oon(*g*) train(*g*)
Open ; closed	*Aberto ; fechado*	e(r)bair'too ; fishah'doo
What is the fare by the hour, cabman ?	*Quanto é o aluguel por hora, cocheiro?*	kwun'too ay oo al-oo-ghel' poor aw're(r), kooshay'roo ?
Put my luggage in the cab	*Ponha a minha bagagem no trem*	pohn'ye(r) e(r) meen'-ye(r) be(r)ghi'zhen(*g*) noo train(*g*)
Drive me to ...	*Conduza-me á ...*	kohndoo'ze(r)-mi ah...
Drive quickly	*Ande depressa*	un'di dipres'se(r)
Drive slower	*Ande mais devagar*	un'di mi'zh div-e(r)gahr'
Stop ! Go on !	*Pare ! Siga !*	pahr'i ! see'ghe(r) !
Wait !	*Espere !*	ishpair'i !
I wish to get out	*Quero sahir*	kair'oo se(r)-eer'

The Omnibus and Tram. *(O Omnibus e Tram-via.)*

English.	Portuguese.	Pronunciation.
The omnibus station	*A estação dos omnibus*	e(r) ishtussow*n*(*g*)' dooz aw'niboozh
Give me a ticket	*Dê-me um bilhete*	deh'-mi oo*n*(*g*) beelyet'i
Conductor	*Conductor*	kohndootohr'
Inside	*Dentro*	den'troo
Outside	*Fóra*	faw're(r)
Platform	*Plataforma*	plut-e(r)fohr'me(r)
Do you go to ...?	*Vae V.Mcê. a...?*	vi vossmussay' e(r)...?
Put me down at...	*Deixe-me em ...,* or *pare em...*	daysh'-mi ai*n*(*g*)..., pah'ri ai*n*(*g*)...
Fares, please	*Paga-se aqui se faz favor*	pah'ghe(r)-si e(r)kee', si fuzh fe(r)-vohr'
What fare to ...?	*Quanto leva para ir a...?*	kwun'too lev'e(r) purr'e(r) eer e(r)...?
Is there room for two inside?	*Caberão dois lá dentro?*	ke(r)berrow*n*(*g*)' doyzh lah den'troo?
"Full"	*"Cheio"*	"shay'oo"
Room for three outside	*Em cima ha lugar para tres*	ai*n*(*g*) see'me(r) ah loo-gahr' pur're(r) trezh
Electric, horse, cable tramway	*Tram-via electrico; puxado por cavallos; a cabo*	trun(*g*)-vee'e(r) i-let'rikoo; pooshah'doo poor ke(r)vahl'loozh; e(r) kah'boo

The Hotel. *(O Hôtel.)*

(See Vocabularies 14, 15 & 18, pages 28 to 31 & 34 to 35.)

Which is the best hotel?	*Qual é o melhor hôtel?*	kwahl ay oo milyawr' aw'tel?
Let us have supper soon	*Traga-nos a ceia sem demora*	trah'ghe(r) - nooz e(r) say'e(r) sai*n*(*g*) di-maw're(r)
Are our rooms ready?	*Estão promptos os nossos quartos?*	ishtow*n*(*g*)' prohn'toozh oozh naw'soozh kwahr'toozh?
I want a bedroom	*Preciso de um quarto de cama*	prissee'zoo di oo*n*(*g*) kwahr'too di kum'me(r)
Let me see the room	*Deixe-me ver o quarto*	daysh'-mi vehr oo kwahr'too

English.	Portuguese.	Pronunciation.
What is the price of this room?	*Quanto custa este quarto?*	kwun'too koosh'te(r) esh'-ti kwahr'too? [roo
That is too dear	*É demasiado caro*	ay di-muzziah'doo kah'-
I want a cheaper one	*Quero um mais barato*	kair'oo oon(*g*) mi'zh be(r)rah'too
Have you a double-bedded room?	*Tem V.Mcê. um quarto com duas camas?*	tain(*g*) vossmussay' oon(*g*) kwahr'too koon(*g*) doo'-uzh kum'muzh?
Are there any letters for me?	*Ha cartas para mim?*	ah kahr'tuzh pur're(r) meen(*g*)? [ne(r)?
Where is the W.C.?	*Onde é a latrina?*	ohn'di ay e(r) le(r)tree'-
Can I have a warm bath?	*Pode preparar-me um banho quente?*	paw'di pripurrahr' - mi oon(*g*) bun'yoo kent'i?
Give me the key of my room	*Dê-me a chave do meu quarto*	deh'-mi e(r) shah'vi doo meh'oo kwahr'too
Bring me some warm water	*Traga-me agua quente*	trah'ghe(r)-mi ah'gwe(r) kent'i
Take my luggage down	*Leve abaixo a minha bagagem*	lev'i e(r)bi'shoo e(r) meen'ye(r) be(r)ghi'-zhen(*g*)
Give me a candle, please	*Dê-me uma vella, se faz favor*	deh'-mi oom'e(r) vel'le(r), si fuzh fe(r)vohr'
We leave early to-morrow	*Partimos amanhã cedo*	Purrtee'moozh e(r)mun-yun(*g*)' seh'doo
Call me at seven	*Chame-me ás sete*	shum'i-mi ahzh set'i

Correspondence. *(Correspondencia.)*

(See Vocabulary 30, page 58.)

English.	Portuguese.	Pronunciation.
I must write a letter	*Devo escrever uma carta*	dev'oo ishkrivehr' oom'-e(r) kahr'te(r)
I want some paper and ink	*Preciso de papel e tinta*	prisee'zoo di pe(r)pel' ee teen'te(r)
Have you any thin note paper?	*Tem V.Mcê. papel fino de formato pequeno?*	tain(*g*) vossmussay' pe(r)-pel' fee'noo di foor-mah'too pi-ken'oo?
Will you give me some?	*Dê-me algum*	deh'-mi ahlgoon(*g*)'
Lend me a sheet	*Empreste-me uma folha*	impresh'ti-mi oom'e(r) fohl'ye(r)
A quire	*Um caderno*	oon(*g*) ke(r)dair'noo

English.	Portuguese.	Pronunciation.
Do you like a hard or soft pen?	*Gosta de uma penna rija ou macia?*	gawsh'te(r) di oom'e(r) pen'ne(r) ree'zhe(r) oh mussee'e(r)?
I like it hard (fine, broad, medium)	*Gosto d'ella rija (fina, larga, mediana)*	gawsh'too del'le(r) ree'-zhe(r) [fee'ne(r), lahr'-ghe(r), middi-un'e(r)]
Is your letter for the post?	*Irá sua carta pelo correio?*	eerah' soo'e(r) kahr' te(r) pel'oo koorray'oo?
What is the day of the month?	*Quantos são hoje?*	kwun'toozh sown(g) oy'-zhi?
To-day is the first	*Hoje é o primeiro*	oy'zhi ay oo preemay'roo
This is the ninth	*Hoje são nove*	oy'zhi sown(g) naw'vi
Seal your letter	*Selle a sua carta*	sel'li e(r) soo'e(r) kahr'-[te(r)
There is no wax	*Não ha lacre*	nown(g) ah lah'kri
Take this letter to the post	*Leve esta carta ao correio*	lev'i esh'te(r) kahr'te(r) ah'oo koorray'oo
Pay the postage	*Pague o porte*	pah'ghi oo pawr'ti
Newspaper wrapper	*Envoltorio de jornaes*	in(g)vohltaw'rioo di zhoorni'zh
Please deliver this by hand	*Queira entregar isto por mão*	kay're(r) intrigahr' ish'-too poor mown(g)

Post-Office and Telegrams. *(O Correio e Telegrammas.)*

(See Vocabulary 31, page 59.)

Stamp of office of origin	*Sello official de origem*	sel'loo awfis'siahl di aw-ree'zhen(g)
Name and address of sender	*Nome e endereço do despachador*	noh'mi i indurress'oo doo dishpe(r)she(r)dohr'
Where is the telegraph (post-) [office?	*Aonde é o telegrapho (correio)?*	e(r)ohn'di ay oo tileg'-ruf-oo (koorray'oo)?
Signature	*Assignatura*	usseene(r)too're(r)
Reply paid	*Resposta paga*	rishpawsh'te(r) pah'ge(r)
Have you any letters (telegrams, newspapers) for Mr. ...?	*Tem V.Mcê. algumas cartas (telegrammas, jornaes) para o Senhor...?*	tain(g) vossmussay' ahl-goo'muzh kahr'tuzh (tiligrum'uzh, zhoor-ni'zh) pur're(r) oo sin-yawr' ...?
Will this letter go to-night?	*Irá esta carta esta noite?*	eerah' esh' te(r) kahr'te(r) esh'te(r) noy'ti?

English.	Portuguese.	Pronunciation.
What is the postage of this letter?	*Quanto é o porte d'esta carta?*	kwun'too ay oo pawr'ti d'esh'te(r) kahr'te(r)?
To register a letter	*Registar uma carta*	rizhishtahr' oom'e(r) kahr'te(r) [zhi
By to-day's post	*Pelo correio de hoje*	pel'oo koorray'oo di oy'-
By return of post	*Pela volta do correio*	pel'e(r) vawl'te(r) doo koorray'oo
I wish to send ...	*Desejo mandar...*	dizezh'oo mun-dahr'...
What is the charge?	*Quanto se paga?*	kwun'too si pah'ghe(r)
The first ten words	*As primeiras dez palavras*	uzh preemay'ruzh dez pe(r)lah'vruzh
Every additional word	*Cada palavra addicional*	kud'e(r) pe(r)lah'vre(r) uddissionahl'
When does the post leave for England?	*Quando parte o correio para Inglaterra?*	kwun'doo pahr'ti oo koorray'oo pur're(r) ingle(r)tair're(r)?
When is the next delivery?	*Quando é a seguinte entrega?*	kwun'doo ay e(r) sigheen'ti intreg'e(r)?
When does the office close?	*Quando fecha o correio?*	kwun'doo fesh'e(r) oo koorray'oo?
I want a Postal Order for...	*Quero um vale para...*	kair'oo oo*n*(*g*) vahl'i pur're(r)...
Payable at the General Post Office, London	*Pagavel no Correio Geral, Londres*	pe(r)gah'vel noo koorray'oo zhurrahl', lohn'drizh
Is the London mail in yet?	*Já chegou a mala de Londres?*	zhah shigoh' e(r) mah'le(r) di lohn'drizh'?
Is there a foreign parcel post?	*Ha correio de encommendas estrangeiro?*	ah koorray'oo di i*n*(*g*)koommen'duzh ishtru*n*(*g*)zhay'roo?
The latest delivery is at ...	*A ultima entrega é ás...horas*	e(r) ool'tim-e(r) intreg'e(r) ay ahzh...aw'ruzh

Breakfast. *(O Almôço.)*

(See Vocabularies 14 & 15, pages 28 & 30.)

Is breakfast ready?	*Está prompto o almôço?* [to	ishtah' prohn'too oo ahlmoh'soo? [prohn'too
Breakfast is ready	*O almôço está promp-*	oo ahlmoh'soo ishtah'
Is the tea made?	*Esta feito o chá?*	ishtah' fay'too oo shah?
Do you drink ...?	*Bebe V.Mcê. ...?*	beb'i vossmussay'...?

English.	Portuguese.	Pronunciation.
This cream is sour	*Esta nata está azeda*	esh'te(r) nah'te(r) ishtah' e(r)zed'e(r)
Will you take ...?	*Toma V.Mcê. ...?*	taw'me(r) vossmussay'...?
These eggs are hard	*Estes ovos estão duros*	esh'tizh aw'voozh ish-town(g)' doo'roozh
Give me the salt	*Dê-me o sal*	deh-mi oo sahl
Pass me ...	*Passe-me ...*	pah'si-mi...
This butter is not fresh	*Esta manteiga não está fresca*	esh'te(r) muntay'ghe(r) nown(g) ishtah' fresh'-ke(r) [me(r)
Bring some more	*Traga mais alguma*	trah'ghe(r) mi'z ahlgoo'-
Is the coffee strong enough?	*Está o café bastante forte?*	ishtah' oo kuffay' be(r)sh-tun'ti fawr'ti?
We want more cups	*Precisamos mais algumas chavanas*	priseezum'oozh mi'z ahl-goo'muzh shah'vun-uzh
Take some more...	*Tome V.Mcê. mais algum*, m. (or *alguma*, f.) ...	taw'mi vossmussay' mi'z ahlgoon(g)' [ahlgoo'-me(r)] ...
A piece of toast	*Uma fatia torrada*	oom'e(r) fe(r)tee'e(r) toor-rah'de(r) [bri
Cold meat	*Carne fria, fiambre*	kahr'ni free'e(r), fi-um'-
A rasher of bacon	*Uma talhada de toucinho*	oom'e(r) tul-yah'de(r) di tohseen'yoo
Coffee with milk	*Café com leite*	kuffay' koon(g) lay'ti
Coffee without milk or cream	*Café só (sem leite ou nata)*	kuffay' saw [sain(g) lay'ti oh nah'te(r)]
Remove the things	*Levante a mesa*	livun'ti e(r) meh'ze(r)

Dinner. *(O Jantar.)*

(See Vocabularies 6, 14 & 15, pages 17, 28 & 30.)

English.	Portuguese.	Pronunciation.
Show me the bill-of-fare	*Mostre-me a lista dos pratos* (or *o menu*)	mawsh'tri-mi e(r) leesh'-te(r) doozh prah'toozh (oo men-oo')
What have you ready?	*O que tem V.Mcê. prompto?*	oo ki tain(g) vossmussay' prohn'too?
What soup will you have?	*Que sôpa quer V.Mcê.?*	ki soh'pe(r) kair voss-mussay'?
Gravy soup	*Sôpa de caldo*	soh'pe(r) di kahl'doo
Have you any...?	*Tem V.Mcê. algum (alguma)...?*	tain(g) vossmussay' ahl-goo'n(g) [ahlgoo'me(r)]

English.	Portuguese.	Pronunciation.
May I give you some fish?	*E servido de peixe?*	ay serrvee'doo di pay'shi?
Fried soles	*Lingoados fritos*	lin(g)gwah'doozh free'toozh
What wine will you have?	*Que vinho quer V.Mcê.?*	ki veen'yoo kair vossmussay'?
Here is the list	*Eis aqui a lista*	ayz e(r)kee' e(r) leesh'te(r)
We shall dine at three o'clock	*Jantaremos as tres horas*	zhunturrem'oozh uzh trez aw'ruzh
Be punctual	*Seja pontual*	sezh'e(r) poontooahl'
Are you hungry, thirsty?	*Tem V.Mcê. fome, sede?*	tain(g) vossmussay' faw'mi, sed'i?
I am very thirsty	*Tenho muita sede*	ten'yoo moo'inte(r) sed'i
What shall I help you to?	*De qual prato posso servil-o?*	di kwahl prah'too paw'soo serrveel'oo?
Which do you prefer?	*Qual prefere V.Mcê?*	kwahl prifair'i vossmussay'?
No, thank you	*Não, muito obrigado*	nown(g), moo'intoo oh-brigah'doo
Help yourself	*Sirva-se V. Mcê. mesmo*	seer've(r)si vossmussay' mezh'moo
I prefer it well-done	*Prefiro-a bem cozida*	prifee'roo-e(r) bain(g) koo-zee'de(r)
It is excellent	*É excellente*	ay ishsellen'ti
Cayenne pepper	*Pimenta cayenna (pimentão)*	peemen'te(r) ke(r)yen'ye(r) [peementown(g)']
Here are spinach and broccoli	*Aqui temos espinafres e brocolos*	e(r)kee' tem'ooz ishpinah'frizh ee braw'kooloozh
Artichokes	*Alcachofas*	ahlke(r)shaw'fuzh
Roast potatoes	*Batatas assadas*	be(r)tah'tuz ussah'duzh
The mustard pot	*O mostardeiro*	oo mooshturrday'roo
Change the plates	*Mude os pratos*	moo'di oozh prah'toozh
Give me a clean fork	*Dê-me um garfo limpo*	deh'-mi oon(g) gahr'foo leem'poo
A clean knife	*Uma faca limpa*	oom'e(r) fah'ke(r) leem'pe(r)
Bring me a glass of water	*Traga-me um copa de agua*	trah'ghe(r)-mi oon(g) kaw'poo di ah'gwe(r)
Give me something to drink	*Dê-me alguma bebida*	deh'-mi ahlgoo'me(r) bi-bee'de(r)
A corkscrew	*Um sacarolhas*	oon(g) se(r)kurrohl'yuzh
This wine tastes of the cork	*Este vinho sabe á rolha*	esh'ti veen'yoo sah'bi ah rohl'ye(r)
It is flat	*Está insipido*	ishtah' een(g)see'pidoo

Tea. *(O Chá.)*

(See Vocabularies 6, 14 & 15, pages 17, 23 & 30.)

English.	Portuguese.	Pronunciation.
Tea is ready	*O chá está prompto*	oo shah ishtah' prohn'too
Will you come?	*Quer vir?*	kair veer?
Pour out the tea	*Deite V.Mcê. o chá*	day'ti vossmussay' oo shah
Bring a saucer	*Traga um pires*	trah'ghe(r) oon(g) pee'-rizh
Ring, if you please	*Toque a campaínha, se faz favor*	taw'ki e(r) kumpe(r)een'-ye(r), si fuzh fe(r)vohr'
A little more milk	*Mais um pouco de leite*	mi'z oon(g) poh'koo di lay'ti
More bread	*Mais pão*	mi'zh pown(g)
A slice of bread and butter	*Uma fatia de pão com manteiga*	oom'e(r) fe(r)tee'e(r) di pown(g) koon(g) mun-tay'ghe(r)
Will you take some cake?	*É servido V.Mcê. de um bocado de bôlo?*	ay serrvee'doo voss-mussay' di oon(g) boo-kah'doo di boh'loo?
A small piece	*Um pedacinho*	oon(g) pidusseen'yoo
Make more toast	*Faça mais algumas torradas*	fah'se(r) mi'z ahlgoo'-muzh toorrah'duzh
This is excellent tea	*Este chá é excellente*	esh'ti shah ay ishsellen'ti

Evening. *(A Noitinha.)*

English.	Portuguese.	Pronunciation.
It is late	*É tarde*	ay tahr'di
It is not late	*Não é tarde*	nown(g) ay tahr'di
It is still early	*Ainda é cedo*	e(r)een'de(r) ay seh'doo
Are you tired—sleepy?	*Está V.Mcê. cansado—com somno?*	ishtah' vossmussay' kun(g)sah'doo—koon(g) soh'noo?
Not at all	*De forma alguma*	di fawr'me(r) ahlgoo'me(r)
Not very	*Não muito*	nown(g) moo'intoo
It is only ten	*São só dez horas*	sown(g) saw dez aw'ruzh
I am sleepy	*Tenho somno*	ten'yoo soh'noo
It is time to go to bed	*São horas de ir para a cama?*	sown(g) aw'ruzh d'eer pur're(r) e(r) kum'e(r)
Is my room ready?	*Está prompta a minha cama?*	ishtah' prohn'te(r) e(r) meen'ye(r) kum'e(r)?
Go and see	*Vá ver*	vah vehr
I shall go to bed	*Vou para a cama*	voh pur're(r) e(r) kum'e(r)
Good night!	*Boanoite!*	boh'e(r)-noy'ti!

The Time. *(A Hora.)*

(See Vocabulary 7, page 20.)

English.	Portuguese.	Pronunciation.
Please tell me the time	*Queira dizer-me que hora é*	kay're(r) dizehr'-mi ki aw're(r) ay
What time is it?	*Que horas são?*	ki aw'ruzh sow*n*(*g*)?
Ten minutes past seven	*São sete horas e dez minutos*	sow*n*(*g*) set'i aw'ruzh i dezh meenoo'tuzh
It has just struck nine	*Acabam de dar as nove horas*	e(r)kah'bu*n*(*g*) di dahr uzh naw'vi aw'ruzh
A quarter past one	*Uma hora e um quarto*	oom'e(r) aw're(r) i oo*n*(*g*) kwahr'too
It is just upon three	*São cerca das tres horas*	sow*n*(*g*) sehr'ke(r) duzh trez aw'ruzh
Half-past four	*Quatro horas e meia*	kwah'troo aw'ruz i may'-[e(r)]
Twenty minutes to six	*Faltam vinte minutos para as seis*	fahl'tu*n*(*g*) veen'ti mee-noo'toozh pur're(r) uzh sayzh
By my watch	*Pelo meu relogio*	pel'oo meh'oo rilaw'zhioo
A quarter to eight	*Falta um quarto para as oito*	fahl'te(r) oo*n*(*g*) kwahr'-too pur're(r) uz oy'too
Exactly 3 o'clock	*Tres horas certas*	trez aw'ruzh sair'tuzh
The clock is striking ...	*Estão dando as ... horas*	ishtow*n*(*g*)' dun'doo uzh ... aw'ruzh
At what time?	*A que hora?*	e(r) ki aw're(r)?
9.0 a.m.	*Nove da manhã*	naw'vi de(r) mun-yu*n*(*g*)'
7.0 p.m.	*Sete da tarde*	set'i de(r) tahr'di

Health. *(A Saúde.)*

(See Vocabulary 18, page 26.)

English.	Portuguese.	Pronunciation.
How are you?	*Como está V.Mcê.?*	koo'moo ishtah' voss-mussay'?
I am very well	*Estou muito bom*	ishtoh' moo'intoo boh*n*(*g*)
— — ill	*Estou doente*	ishtoh' dooen'ti
— — not very well	*Não me acho bom*	now*n*(*g*) mi ah'shoo [boh*n*(*g*)]
I hope you will soon be better	*Estimarei as suas melhoras brevemente*	ishteemurray' uzh soo'-uzh mil-yaw'ruzh brev-vimen'ti [bai*n*(*g*)?]
Do you sleep well?	*Dorme V.Mcê. bem?*	dawr'mi vossmussay'
Pretty well, thank you	*Menos mal, agradecido*	men'oozh mahl, e(r)-gre(r)di-see'doo

English.	Portuguese.	Pronunciation.
I have a headache	*Tenho dôres de cabeça*	ten' yoo doh'rizh di ke(r)-bess'e(r)
— — a sore throat	— — *de garganta*	— — di gurrgun'te(r)
— — caught a chill	*Apanhei um resfrio (calefrio)*	e(r)pun-yay' oo*n*(*g*) rish-free'oo (kullifree'oo)
I feel sick	*Estou agoniado*	ishtoh' e(r)gooniah'doo
Send for a doctor	*Mande buscar um medico*	mun'di booshkahr' oo*n*(*g*) med'ikoo
I want to see a ...	*Desejo ver um...*	dizeh'zhoo vehr oo*n*(*g*)...
She has a cough	*Ella tem tosse*	el'le(r) tai*n*(*g*) tawss'i
She is hoarse	*Está rouca*	ishtah' roh'ke(r)
Where is there a chemist's shop?	*Aonde ha uma botica?*	e(r)ohn'di ah oom'e(r) bootee'ke(r)?
How much is the doctor's fee for a visit?	*Quanto leva o medico por visita?*	kwun'too levv'e(r) oo med'ikoo poor vizee'-te(r)?
Have this prescription made up	*Mande preparar esta receita*	mun'di pripurrahr' esh'-te(r) rissay'te(r)
One tablespoonful three times a day	*Uma colherada trez vezes por dia*	oom'e(r) kool-yerrah'-de(r) trezh vezezh poor dee'e(r)
To be taken after each meal	*Toma-se depois de cada comida*	taw'me(r)-si dipoy'zh di kud'e(r) koomee'de(r)
Shake the bottle	*Agite o frasco*	e(r)zhee'ti oo frahsh'koo
Poison!	*Veneno!*	vin-en'oo!
Outward application only	*Para applicação exterior sómente*	pur're(r) uppleeke(r)-sow*n*(*g*)' ishterriohr' sawmen'ti

In Town. *(A Cidade.)*

(See Vocabularies 10, 21 & 30, pages 22, 40 & 57.)

English.	Portuguese.	Pronunciation.
Where shall we go?	*Aonde iremos?*	e(r)ohn'di eerem'oozh?
Which is the way to...?	*Qual é o caminho para...?*	kwahl ay oo kummeen'-yoo pur're(r)...?
Where does this road lead?	*Aonde vae dar este caminho?*	e(r)ohn'di vi dahr esh'ti kummeen'yoo?
Straight before you	*Em linha direita*	ai*n*(*g*) leen'ye(r) diray'-te(r)
To the right	*Á direita*	ah diray'te(r)
— — left	*Á esquerda*	ah ishkair'de(r)
About a mile	*Cerca de uma milha*	serr'ke(r) di oom'e(r) meel'ye(r)

English.	Portuguese.	Pronunciation.
Go up the street	*Suba V.Mcê. a rua*	soo'be(r) vossmussay' e(r) roo'e(r)
Is it far from here?	*É longe d'aqui?*	ay loh*n*(*g*)'zhi d'e(r)kee'?
How far is it to...?	*Qual é a distancia até...?*	kwahl ay e(r) dishtu*n*(*g*)'-sie(r) e(r)tay'...?
Where can I get an omnibus to...?	*Aonde posso tomar um omnibus para...?*	e(r)ohn'di paw'soo too-mahr' oo*n*(*g*) aw'ni-boozh pur're(r)...?
Go quickly	*Vá depressa*	vah dipres'se(r)
— slowly	*Vá devagar*	vah divve(r)gahr'
Straight on	*Em linha recta*	ai*n*(*g*) leen'ye(r) ray'te(r)
Let us go	*Vamo-nos*	vummoo'-noozh
Show me the way	*Indique-me o caminho*	indeek'i - mi oo ke(r)-meen'yoo
Turn to the right	*Volte á direita*	vawl'ti ah diray'te(r)
Keep to the left	*Segue á esquerda*	seg'i ah ishkair'de(r)
Second turning to the right	*A segunda travessa á direita*	e(r) sigoon'de(r) tre(r)-vess'e(r) ah diray'te(r)
Take the first to the left and the second to the right	*Tome a primeira á esquerda e a segunda á direita*	taw'mi e(r) preemay're(r) ah ishkair'de(r) i e(r) si-goon'de(r) ah diray'te(r)
Cross the road	*Atravesse a rua*	e(r)tre(r)ves'si e(r) roo'-e(r)
In what street is...?	*Em que rua é...?*	ai*n*(*g*) ki roo'e(r) ay..?
Is this the way to...?	*É este o caminho para...?*	ay esh'ti oo ke(r)meen'-yoo pur're(r)...?
In what street are the best shops?	*Em que rua ha as melhores lojas?*	ai*n*(*g*) ki roo'e(r) ah uzh mil-yawr'izh law'zhuzh?
Please direct me the nearest way to ...	*Sirva-se indicar me o caminho mais curto para...?*	seer've(r)-si indikahr'-mi oo ke(r)meen'yoo mizh koor'too pur're(r)..?
Which omnibus [tram] must I take for...?	*Que omnibus (tram-via) devo tomar para...?*	ki aw'niboozh [trah*n*(*g*)-vee'e(r)] dev'oo too-mahr' pur're(r)...?
Do you know Mr. F.?	*Conhece V.Mcê. o Senhor F.?*	koon-yess'i vossmussay' oo sinyawr' F.?
I don't know any-one of that name	*Não conheço nin-guem d'esse nome*	now*n*(*g*) koon-yess'oo nee*n*(*g*)ghai*n*(*g*)' d'ess'i noh'mi
I know him very well	*Conheço-o muito bem*	koon-yess'oo-oo moo'in-too bai*n*(*g*)
Who is he?	*Quem é elle?*	kai*n*(*g*) ay el'li?

English.	Portuguese.	Pronunciation.
He is an old friend of mine	*É velho amigo meu*	ay vel'yoo e(r)mee'goo meh'oo
Where does he live?	*Aonde mora-elle?*	e(r)ohn'di maw're(r) el'li?
Close by	*Aqui perto*	e(r)kee' pair'too
Can you direct me to a good hotel?	*Pode V.Mcê. indicar-me um bom hôtel?*	paw'di vossmussay' indeekahr'-mi oo*n*(*g*) boh*n*(*g*) aw'tel?
Is Mr. F. (Mrs. F.) at home?	*Está o Senhor F. (a Senhora F.) em casa?*	ishtah' oo sinyawr' F. [e(r) sinyaw're(r) F.] ai*n*(*g*) kah'ze(r)?
Good morning	*Bons dias*	boh*n*(*g*)zh dee'uzh
How do you do?	*Como passou?*	koh'moo pe(r)ssoh'?
Very well	*Muito bem*	moo'intoo bai*n*(*g*)
I am very well	*Estou muito bom*	ishtoh moo'intoo boh*n*(*g*)
I must go	*Tenho de ir-me embora*	ten'yoo di eer'-mi imbaw're(r)
Good-bye, farewell	*Adeus, passe muito bem*	e(r)deh'oozh, pah'si moo'intoo bai*n*(*g*)
I wish you good morning	*Desejo-lhe muito bons dias*	dez-ezh'ool-yi moo'intoozh boh*n*(*g*)zh dee'uzh
Good evening	*Boas tardes*	boh'uzh tahr'dizh
Good night	*Boas noites*	boh'uzh noy'tizh

Shopping. *(A Loja.)*

(See Vocabularies 6, 7, 14, 15, 16, 18 & 21.)

English.	Portuguese.	Pronunciation.
How much?	*Quanto?*	kwun'too?
That is too much	*Isso é demais*	ee'soo ay dimi'zh
What is the price?	*Qual é o preço?*	kwahl ay oo press'oo?
Will you send them at once?	*Tenha a bondade de envial-os em seguida*	ten'ye(r) e(r) bohndah'di di i*n*(*g*)viah'looz ai*n*(*g*) si-ghee'de(r)
I wish to buy...	*Desejo comprar...*	dez-ezh'oo kohmprahr'...
I will take this	*Tomarei este-a isto*	toomurray' esh'ti-e(r) [e(r)... eesh'too
Send them to...	*Remetta-os para...*	rimet'te(r)-oozh purr'e(r)...
I want some calico	*Desejo algum morim*	dizezh'oo ahlgoo*n*(*g*)' mooree*n*(*g*)'
I should like to see some ribbons	*Quero ver algumas fitas*	kair'oo vehr ahlgoom'uzh feet'uzh

English.	Portuguese.	Pronunciation.
This colour is too dark; light	*Esta côr é demasiado escura; clara*	esh'te(r) kohr ay dimuzziah'doo ishkoo're(r); klah're(r)
Have you any narrower, broader?	*Tem V.Mcê. algumas mais estreitas, largas?*	tain(*g*) vossmussay' ahlgoom'uzh mi'zh ishtray'tuzh, lahr'guzh?
What is this a yard?	*Quanto custa isto a vara?*	kwun'too koosh'te(r) eesh'too e(r) vah're(r)?
It is faded	*Está desbotado*	ishtah' dizhbootah'doo
Show me some dress material	*Mostre-me alguma fazenda para vestidos*	mawsh'tri-mi ahlgoom'e(r) fuzzen'de(r) purr'e(r) vishtee'doozh
Some gloves	*Algumas luvas*	ahlgoom'uzh loo'vuzh
— others	*Outras*	oh'truzh
Not so fine	*Não tão fina*	nown(*g*) town(*g*) feen'e(r)
This will do [silk	*Esta serve [troz*	esh'te(r) sair'vi [trawzh'
A skein of sewing-	*Uma meada de re-*	oom'e(r) miah'de(r) di ri-
Mixed pins; needles	*Alfinetes sortidos; agulhas*	ahlfinet'izh soortee'doozh; e(r)gool'yuzh
Tape	*Fita de algodão*	fee'te(r) di ahlgoodown(*g*)'
A bodkin	*Uma agulheta*	oom'e(r) e(r)gool-yet'e(r)
What are they a pair?	*Quanto custam ao par?*	kwun'too koosh'tun(*g*) ah'oo pahr?
It is too dear	*É muito caro*	ay moo'intoo kah'roo
Try on these	*Prove V.Mcê. estas*	praw'vi vossmussay' esh'tuzh
They fit you very well [with me	*Assentam-lhe muito bem*	us-sen'tun(*g*)l-yi moo'intoo bain(*g*)
I will take them	*Leval-as-hei comigo*	livahl'uz-ay koomee'goo
Send this home directly	*Mande tudo isto para minha casa quanto antes*	mun'di too'doo eesh'too pur're(r) meen'ye(r) kah'ze(r) kwun'too un'tizh
Make out my bill	*Tire-me a conta*	teer'-mi e(r) kohn'te(r)

The Dressmaker. *(A Modista.)*

(See Vocabulary 16, page 31.)

Here is the dressmaker	*Eis aqui a modista*	ayz e(r)kee' e(r) moodeesh'te(r)
Tell her to wait	*Diga-lhe que espere*	dee'ghul-yi ki ishpair'i
Show her in	*Faça-a entrar*	fah'se(r)-e(r) intrahr'

English.	Portuguese.	Pronunciation.
Have you brought my dress?	*Traz-me V.Mcê. o meu vestido*	trahzh'-mi vossmussay' oo meh'oo vishtee'doo?
Here it is	*Eil-o aqui [tal-o?*	ay'loo e(r)kee' [tahl'oo?
Will you try it on?	*Queira experimen-*	kay're(r) ishperrimen-
It fits you very well	*Assenta-lhe muito bem*	ussen'te(r)l-yi moo'intoo bain(g)
The sleeves are not wide enough	*As mangas não estão bastante largas*	uzh mun(g)'guzh nown(g) ishtown(g)' be(r)sh-tun'ti lahr'guzh
The skirt is too narrow	*A saia está muito estreita*	e(r) si'e(r) ishtah' moo'-intoo ishtray'te(r)
Add another breadth	*Ajunte-lhe outro tanto de largura*	e(r)zhoon'til-yi oh'troo tun'too di lurrgoo're(r)
It is short-waisted	*Tem a cintura alta*	tain(g) e(r) seentoo're(r) ahl'te(r) [bi'she(r)
It is long-waisted	*Tem a cintura baixa*	tain(g) e(r) seentoo're(r)
Make all these alterations	*Faça todas estas alterações*	fah'se(r) toh'duzh esh'-tuzh ahlterrussoy'n(g)zh
What trimming would you put on?	*Que guarnição vae V.Mcê. pôr-lhe?*	ki gurnissown(g)' vi voss-mussay' pohr'l-yi?
Light blue ribbon	*Fita azul clara*	fee'te(r) e(r)zool' klah'-re(r)
When can I have it?	*Quando tel-o-hei?*	kwun'doo tel'oo-ay?
You shall have it on Saturday	*Deverá tel-o no Sabbado*	di-verrah' tel'oo noo sah'-bud-oo
Without fail	*Sem falta*	sain(g) fahl'te(r)
Don't disappoint me	*Não me falte V.Mcê.*	nown(g) mi fahl'ti voss-mussay'

The Shoemaker. (*O Sapateiro.*)

English.	Portuguese.	Pronunciation.
I wish to see some shoes — boots — slippers	*Desejo ver uns sapatos — umas botinas — umas chinelas*	dizezh'oo vehr oon(g)zh se(r)pah'toozh—oom'-uzh booteen'uzh — oom'uzh sheenel'uzh
Ladies', gentlemen's, children's	*Para senhoras, homens, creanças*	pur're(r) sinyaw'ruzh, aw'men(g)zh, kri-un(g)'suzh
The soles are rather thick, thin	*As solas são um pouco grossas—delgadas*	uzh saw'luzh sown(g) oon(g) poh'koo graw'-suzh—delgah'duzh.

English.	Portuguese.	Pronunciation.
They are too tight, short, long	*Estão muito apertadas, curtas, compridas*	ishtow*n*(*g*)' moo'intoo e(r)pertah'duzh, koor'tuzh, kohmpree'duzh
The heels are too high	*Os tacões estão muito altos*	oozh te(r)koy'*n*(*g*)zh ishtow*n*(*g*)' moo'intoo ahl'toozh
I cannot get my foot in	*Não posso metter o pé*	now*n*(*g*) pawss'oo mettehr' oo pay
Here is a shoe-horn	*Eis aqui um calçador*	ayz e(r)kee' oo*n*(*g*) kahlse(r)dohr'
They hurt my heel (toes, instep)	*Ferem-me no calcanhar (nos dedos—no peito do pé*	fair'i*n*(*g*)-mi noo kahlkunyahr'(noozh ded'oozh—noo pay'too doo pay)
I cannot walk in them	*Não posso andar com ellas*	now*n*(*g*) pawss'oo undahr' koo*n*(*g*) el'luzh
Take my measure	*Tome a minha medida*	taw'mi e(r) meen'ye(r) midee'de(r)
I must have them as soon as possible	*Precisalos-hei quanto antes*	prisseezah'looz-ay kwun'too un'tizh

The Laundress. *(A Lavadeira.)*

(See Vocabulary 16, p. 31, and Washing List, p. 33.)

English.	Portuguese.	Pronunciation.
This is too limp	*Isto está muito frouxo*	eesh'too ishtah' moo'intoo froh'shoo
You don't put enough starch in	*V. Mcê. não usa gomma sufficiente*	vossmussay' now*n*(*g*) oo'ze(r) goh'me(r) sooffissien'ti
I miss a collar	*Falta-me um collarinho*	fahl'te(r)-mi oo*n*(*g*) koollurreen'yoo
See how badly that is ironed, starched	*Veja como isso está mal passado a ferro, mal engommado*	vezh'e(r) koo'moo ee'soo ishtah' mahl pe(r)ssah'doo e(r) fair'roo, mahl i*n*(*g*)goommah'doo
You have scorched this dress	*V.Mcê. chamuscou este vestido*	vossmussay' she(r)moosh'koh esh'ti vishtee'doo
You put too much blue in my linen	*V.Mcê. põe muito azul na minha roupa*	vossmussay' poy*n*(*g*) moo'intoo e(r)zool' ne(r) meen'ye(r) roh'pe(r)
This is not my handkerchief	*Este lenço não é meu*	esh'ti le*n*(*g*)'soo now*n*(*g*) ay meh'oo

English.	Portuguese.	Pronunciation.
You have torn this dress [it?	*V.Mcê. rasgou este vestido*	vossmussay' ruzh'goh esh'ti vishtee'doo [oo?
When can I have	*Quando posso tel-o ?*	kwun'doo pawss'oo tel'-
Have you your bill?	*Traz V.Mcê. a sua conta?*	trahzh vossmussay' e(r) soo'e(r) kohn'te(r)?
I will pay you	*Eu lhe pagarei*	eh'ool-yi puggurray'
I want this linen washed	*Quero que se lave esta roupa*	kair'oo ki si lah'vi esh'-te(r) roh'pe(r)
Please return this linen on ...	*Sirva-se devolver esta roupa em...*	seer've(r)-si divawlvehr' esh'te(r) roh'pe(r) ain(*g*)..
You must bring back this list	*Esta lista deve V.Mcê. devolver-me*	esh'te(r) leesh'te(r) dev'i vossmussay' divawl-vehr'-mi

Cycling Phrases. (*Phrases para os Bicyclistas.*)

(See Vocabulary 20, page 51.)

English.	Portuguese.	Pronunciation.
I want my machine	*Necessito a minha machina*	nissessee'too e(r) meen'-ye(r) mah'kin-e(r)
Fitted with all accessories	*Disposta com todos os accessorios*	dishpawsh'te(r) koon(*g*) toh'dooz ooz ukses-saw'rioozh
I wish to hire ...	*Desejo alugar...*	diz-ezh'oo e(r)loogahr'...
By the hour	*Por horas*	poor aw'ruzh
By the day	*Pelo dia inteiro*	pel'oo dee'e(r) eentay'roo
What are your terms?	*Quaes são as suas condições de aluguel?*	kwi'zh sown(*g*) uzh soo'-uzh kohndissoy'n(*g*)zh di e(r)loo-ghel'?
Have you a cycle shelter?	*Tem V. Mcê. um abrigo para bicycletas?*	tain(*g*) vossmussay' oon(*g*) ub-ree'goo pur're(r) beeseeklet'uzh?
To tighten—loosen—a nut	*Apertar—desapertar—uma porca*	up-errtahr'—diz-upperr-tahr'—oom'e(r) pawr'-ke(r)
Are the roads good or bad?	*Estão as estradas boas ou más?*	ishtown(*g*)' uz ishtrah'-duzh boh'uzh oh mahzh?
The chain is off	*Cahiu a cadeia*	ke(r)ee'oo e(r) ke(r)-day'e(r)
I must inflate my tyres	*Devo inflar os meus aros de borracha*	dev'oo een(*g*)flahr' oozh meh'ooz ah'roozh di boorrah'she(r)

English.	Portuguese.	Pronunciation.
I have broken ...	*Quebrei...*	kibray'...
Are you ready?	*Está V.Mcê. prompto?*	ishtah' vossmussay' prohn'too?
We will start at ...	*Partiremos ás...*	purrteerem'oozh ahzh...
Ring your bell	*Toque a sua campainha*	taw'ki e(r) soo'e(r) kumpe(r)een'ye(r)
My tyre is punctured	*Está punctuado o meu aro*	ishtah' poonktooah'doo oo meh'oo ah'roo
Stop! Look out!	*Pare! Cuidado!*	pahr'i! kooeedah'doo!
Don't go so fast	*Não va tão depressa*	nown(g) vah town(g) dipres'se(r)
Make haste!	*Apressa-se!*	up-res'se(r)-si!
Keep straight on	*Siga V. Mcê. direito*	see'ghe(r) vossmussay' diray'too
We must light up	*Temos de acender a luz*	tem'oozh di ussendehr' e(r) loozh
My lamp requires a new wick	*Minha lanterna precisa d'uma torcida nova*	meen'ye(r) luntair'ne(r) prisee'ze(r) d'oom'e(r) toorsee'de(r) naw've(r)
Have you a road guide?	*Tem V. Mcê. um mappa do caminho?*	tain(g) vossmussay' oon(g) mah'pe(r) doo ke(r)-meen'yoo?
Yes; which one do you require?	*Sim, tenho; qual deseja V.Mcê.?*	seen(g), ten'yoo; kwahl dizezh'e(r) vossmussay'?
The one for Lisbon and environs	*Um de Lisboa e seus arredores*	oon(g) di leezhboh'e(r) ee seh'ooz urredoh'rizh
I want my machine cleaned	*Preciso que me limpem a machina*	priseez'oo ki mi leem'-pen(g) e(r) mah'kin-e(r)
Where can I get my bicycle mended?	*Aonde poderiam concertar a minha machina?*	e(r)ohn'di pooderree'-un(g) kohn(g)serrtahr' e(r) meen'ye(r) mah'-kin-e(r)?
Can you repair this for me?	*Pode V.Mcê. concertar-me isto?*	paw'di vossmussay' kohn-serrtahr'-mi eesh'too?
How long will it take?	*Quanto tempo levará?*	kwun'too tem'poo livur-rah'?
I am a member of the London Cyclists' Touring Club; here is my ticket	*Sou socio do "London Cyclists' Touring Club"; eis aqui o meu bilhete*	soh saw'sioo doo "London Cyclists' Touring Club"; aiz e(r)kee' oo meh'oo beel-yet'i

Motoring Phrases. (*Phrases Automobiliarios.*)

(For Vocabulary see p. 54; see also Cycling, pages 51 to 53 & 113 to 114.)

English.	Portuguese.	Pronunciation.
Have you examined my speed-changing gear?	*Já examinou o apparelho de mudar a velocidade?*	zhah izum'inoh oo uppurrel'yoo di moodahr' e(r) vilawssidah'di?
Replace my brake	*Ponha um travão novo*	pohn'ye(r) oon(*g*) tre(r)-vown(*g*)' noh'voo
The clutch is out of order	*A roda livre (embrayage) não funciona*	e(r) raw'de(r) leev'ri [imbre(r)-yahzh'] nown(*g*) foon(*g*)sioh'ne(r)
I want a carburator for voiturette	*Preciso de um carburador para voiturette*	prisee'zoo di oon(*g*) kurrboore(r)dohr' pur're(r) vwahtooret'i
My back spring is broken	*Quebrou-se a minha molla trazeira*	kibroh'-si e(r) meen'ye(r) mawl'le(r) tre(r)zay're(r)
Change it	*Troque-a*	traw'ki-e(r)
A pinion is wanted for the small axle	*Falta uma cavilha para o eixo pequeno*	fahl'te(r) oom'e(r) ke(r)-veel'ye(r) pur're(r) oo ay'shoo piken'oo
I have lost my horn (hooter)	*Perdi a minha buzina*	perrdee' e(r) meen'ye(r) boozee'ne(r)
Have you an accumulator—four volts?	*Tem V. Mcê. um accumulador—de quatro voltes?*	tain(*g*) vossmussay' oon(*g*) ukkoomoole(r)dohr' — di kwah'troo vawl'tizh?
You must fix the radiator to the frame	*V. Mcê. deve fixar o radiador na armação*	vossmussay' dev'i feex-ah(r)' oo ruddie(r)dohr' ne(r) ahrme(r)sown(*g*)'
Give me a petrol tube	*Dê-me um tubo para petroleo*	deh-mi oon(*g*) too'boo pur' re(r) pitraw'lioo
Give me an automobile map on cloth	*Dê-me um mappa forrado de panno, para automovel*	deh-mi oon(*g*) mahp'pe(r) foorrah'doo di pun'-noo pur're(r) owtoo-maw'vel
What is the power of this motor?	*De que força é este motor?*	di ki fawhr'se(r) ay esh'-ti mootohr'?
This is an eight-horse-power engine	*Esta machina é da força de oito cavallos*	esh'te(r) mah'kin-e(r) ay de(r) fohr'se(r) di oy'-too ke(r)vahl'loozh
Is it a good hill-climber?	*Sobe bem os outeiros?*	saw'bi bain(*g*) ooz oh-tay'roozh?

Photographic Phrases. *(Phrases photographicas.)*

(For Vocabulary see p. 55.)

English.	Portuguese.	Pronunciation.
Must permission be obtained to photograph?	*Para tomar photographias, será preciso obter licença?*	pur're(r) toomahr' footoogre(r)fee'uzh, si-rah' prisee'zoo obtehr' leesen(*g*)'se(r)?
I wish to take the interior	*Desejo photographar o interior*	dez-ezh'oo footoogre(r)fahr' oo interriohr'
What exposure must I give it?	*Quanto tempo devo expôl-a?*	kwun'too tem'poo dev'oo ishpoh'le(r)?
The light is too strong	*A luz é muito forte*	e(r) looz ay moo'intoo fawr'ti [koo
It is out of focus	*Está fora do foco*	ishtah' faw're(r) doo faw'-
What size of plate do you use?	*Que tamanho de chapa emprega V.Mcê.?*	ki te(r)mun'yoo di shah'pe(r) impreg'e(r) vossmussay'?
I only use quarter-plate	*Emprego só um quarto de chapa*	impreg'oo saw oon(*g*) kwahr'too di shah'pe(r)
Have you a dark room?	*Tem V.Mcê. uma camara escura?*	tai(*n*)*g* vossmussay' oom'e(r) kum'urre(r) ishkoo're(r)?
I want to develop some plates	*Quero revelar umas chapas*	kair'oo rivvelahr' oom'uzh shah'puzh
What a beautiful photograph!	*Que bella photographia!*	ki bel'le(r) footoogre(r)fee'e(r)!
It is a perfect picture	*É uma reproducção perfeita*	ay oom'e(r) riproodoosown(*g*)' perrfay'te(r)
This plate is spoilt	*A chapa estragou-se*	e(r) shah'pe(r) ishtre(r)goh'si
That is due to over-exposure	*Isso é devido a ter sido demasiadamente exposta*	ee'soo ay divee'doo e(r) tehr see'doo dimuzziahde(r)men'ti ishpawsh'te(r)
I am going to print more copies	*Vou imprimir mais copias*	voh imprimeer' mi'zh kaw'pi-uzh
This was spoilt in the printing	*Esta estragou-se no imprimir*	esh'te(r) ishtre(r)goh'si noo imprimeer'
The grouping is very good	*O agrupamento está bem*	oo e(r)groope(r)men'too ishtah' bain(*g*)
I have secured some fine views	*Consegui algumas bellas vistas*	kohn(*g*)si-ghee' ahlgoo'muzh bel'luzh veesh'- [tuzh

Commercial and Trading. *(Commerçio e Negocio.)*

(For Vocabulary see pages 46 to 51.)

English.	Portuguese.	Pronunciation.
Send in my account	*Mande-me a sua conta*	mun'di-mi e(r) soo'e(r) kohn'te(r)
I am leaving to-[morrow	*Partirei ámanhã*	purrteeray' ahmun-[yun(g)'
You have over-charged me	*V.Mcê. levou-me demais*	vossmussay' livoh'-mi dimi'zh
Give me a receipt	*Dê-me um recibo*	deh'-mi oon(g) risee'boo
The firm has failed	*A firma falliu*	e(r) feer'me(r) fe(r)llee'oo
What are the assets —the liabilities?	*Qual é o activo —o passivo?*	kwahl ay oo ahtee'voo —oo pe(r)ssee'voo?
Show me a balance-sheet	*Mostre-me o balancete*	mawsh'tri-mi oo be(r)-lun(g)set'i
There is an error in your account	*Ha engano na sua conta*	ah in(g)gun'oo ne(r) soo'-e(r) kohn'ter
My samples are delayed	*As minhas amostras demoram-se*	uzh meen'yuzh e(r)-mawsh'truzh dimaw'-run(g)-si
I want to get them through the Custom House	*Desejo despachal-as na alfandega*	dizezh'oo dishpe(r)-shahl'uzh ne(r) ahlfun'di-ghe(r)
I want a detailed statement	*Quero uma relação detalhada*	kair'oo oom'e(r) rille(r)-sown(g)' ditul-yah'-de(r)
I shall send in a claim	*Vou apresentar uma reclamação*	voh e(r)prizentahr' oom'-e(r) riklumme(r)-sown(g)'
Can I insure my luggage?	*Poderei effectuar o seguro sobre a minha bagagem?*	pooderay' iffetooahr' oo sigoo'roo soh'bri e(r) meen'ye(r) be(r)-ghi'zhen(g)?
What is the rate? —the charge?	*Qual é a taxa?—o importe?*	kwahl ay e(r) tah'she(r)? —oo impawr'ti?
Will you accept a bill?	*Quer V.Mcê. acceitar uma letra?*	kair vossmussay' us-say-tahr' oom'e(r) let're(r)?
At three months	*A tres mezes*	e(r) trezh mez'ezh
Send by fast train	*Mande pelo comboio rapido*	mun'di pel'oo kohmboy'-oo rah'pidoo
They can go by goods train	*Poderão seguir pelo comboio de mercadorias*	pooderrown(g)' si-gheer' pel'oo kohmboy'oo di merrke(r)doo-ree'uzh

English.	Portuguese.	Pronunciation.
What dividend is declared?	*Que dividendo foi declarado?*	ki dividen'doo foy dik-lurrah'doo?
Your luggage is liable to duty	*A sua bagagem é sugeita a direitos*	e(r) soo'e(r) be(r)ghi'-zhen(*g*) ay soo-zhay'-te(r) e(r) diray'toozh
This cheque needs endorsing	*Este cheque precisa ser endossado*	esh'ti shaik'i prisee'ze(r) sehr indoossah'doo
Have you declared the value?	*Já declarou o valor?*	zhah diklurroh' oo ve(r)lohr'?
I will prepay the carriage	*O carreto eu franquiarei*	oo kurret'oo eh'oo frun(*g*)'ki-urray
I have a letter of introduction	*Tenho uma carta de recommendação*	ten'yoo oom'é(r) kahr'-te(r) di rikoomende(r)-sown(*g*)'
Give me your estimate	*Dê-me a sua avaliação*	deh'-mi e(r) soo'e(r) uv-ulli-ussown(*g*)'
Quote me a price	*Queira cotar-me um preço*	kay're(r) kootahr'-mi oon(*g*) press'oo

Changing Money. *(Cambiar Dinheiro.)*

Where can I get money changed?	*Aonde poderei cambiar dinheiro?*	e(r)ohn'di pooderay' kumbiahr' dinyair'oo?
Where is the bank (a money-changer)?	*Aonde é o banco (um cambista)?*	e(r)ohn'di ay oo bun(*g*)'-koo [oon(*g*) kumbeesh'-te(r)]?
I want change for a five-pound note	*Preciso trôco d'uma nota de cinca libras?*	prisee'zoo troh'koo d'oom'e(r) naw'te(r) di seen(*g*)'koo lee'bruzh
Will you give me Portuguese money?	*Quer V.Mcê. dar-me moeda portugueza?*	kair vossmussay' dahr'-mi moo-ed'e(r) poorr-too-ghez'e(r)?
What is the exchange on English money?	*Qual é o cambio sobre moeda ingleza?*	kwahl ay oo kum'bioo soh'bri moo-ed'e(r) in-glez'e(r)?
Will you change me these sovereigns?	*Queira trocar-me estas libras?*	kay're(r) trookahr'-mi esh'tuzh lee'bruzh?
Will you cash this cheque for me?	*Quer V.Mcê. trocar-me este cheque?*	kair vossmussay' trook-ahr'-mi esh'ti shaik'i?

English.	Portuguese.	Pronunciation.
Please give me gold and silver, not paper money	*Faça favor de dar-me ouro e prata, e não papel*	fah'se(r) fe(r)vohr' di dahr'-mi oh'roo ee prah'te(r), ee nown(g) pe(r)pel'
A bill of exchange	*Uma letra de cambio*	oom'e(r) let're(r) di kum'-bioo
It is payable at [sight	*É pagavel á vista*	ay pe(r)gah'vel ah veesh'-[te(r)
Give me the amount in reis	*Dê-me a importancia em reis*	deh'-mi e(r) impoor-tun(g)'sie(r) ain(g) rayzh
Have you an agent in ...?	*Tem V.Mcê. agente em...?*	tain(g) vossmussay' e(r)-zhen'ti ain(g)...?

MONEY. (*Numerario.*)

Portuguese Money, with English & American Equivalents.

NOTE.—These equivalents are subject to fluctuations in the rate of exchange. The monetary unit is the *milreis* (thousand *reis*).

GOLD COINAGE. (*Moedas de Ouro.*)

PORTUGUESE.		English £	s.	d.	American dols.	cents.
Corôa	(10 *milreis*)	2	4	2	... 10	70
Meia Corôa	(5 *milreis*)	1	2	1	... 5	35
Quinto de Corôa	(2 *milreis*)		8	10	... 2	14
Decimo de Corôa	(1 *milreis*)		4	5	... 1	7

SILVER. (*Moedas de Prata.*)

		s.	d.	cents.
Cinco (5) *Tostões*	(500 *reis*)	2	2½	... 53
Dois (2) ,,	(200 *reis*)		10¼	... 21
Um (1) *Tostão*	(100 *reis*)		5	... 10
Meio (½) ,,	(50 *reis*)		2½	... 5

BRONZE. (*Moedas de Cobre.*)

		d.	cents.
Vintem	(20 *reis*)	1	... 2
Dez reis	(10 *reis*)	0½	... 1
Cinco reis	(5 *reis*)	0¼	... —

PAPER. (*Papel.*)

NOTES of 50, 100, 200, 500 *reis*, 1 *milreis*, and upwards are issued. The value of the paper *milreis* is about 3s. 9d.

English & American Money, with Portuguese Equivalents.

ENGLISH.		PORTUGUESE.	AMERICAN.		PORTUGUESE.
Pound (£1) ...	=	4 *milreis* 530 *reis*	100 dollars ...	=	93 *milreis* 396 *reis*
Half-crown (2s. 6d.)	=	... 565 ,,	10 ,, ...	=	9 ,, 340 ,,
Florin (2s.) ...	=	... 453 ,,	1 dollar ...	=	... 934 ,,
Shilling (1s.) ...	=	... 225 ,,	50 cents ...	=	... 467 ,,
Sixpence (6d.) ...	=	... 113 ,,	10 ,, ...	=	... 93 ,,
Penny (1d.) ...	=	... 20 ,,	5 ,, ...	=	... 46 ,,

WEIGHTS AND MEASURES. *(Pesos e Medidas.)*

The METRIC SYSTEM is the legal standard, but certain of the old Weights and Measures are still in use. The following table shows the essential (decimal) character of the system.

Parts.	Length.	Capacity.	Weight.
100th	centimetro	centilitro	centigramma
10th	decimetro	decilitro	decigramma
1	METRO (unit)	LITRO (unit)	GRAMMA (unit)
10	decametro	decalitro	decagramma
100	hectometro	hectolitro	hectogramma
1,000	kilometro	kilolitro	kilogramma

MEASURES OF LENGTH. *(Medidas de Comprimento.)*

English.	Portuguese.
1 inch	= 2·5399 *centimetros (cm.)*
1 foot (12 in.)	= 30 *centimetros*
1 yard (3 ft.)	= 91 *cm.* ($\frac{9}{10}$ *metro*)
1 furlong (220 yds.)	= 201 *metros*
1 mile (1760 yds.)	= 1 *kilometro* [610 *metros*
5 miles	= 8 *kilometros*

Portuguese.	English.
1 *centimetro*	= 0·394 inches
30 *centimetros*	= 1 foot
1 *metro*	= 3 ft. 3 in. (39·37 in.)
1 *hectometro*	= 109 yards 1 foot
1 *kilometro*	= 1093 yards 2 feet
5 *kilometros*	= 3 miles 220 yards

NOTE.—The Portuguese measures *vara, pé* and *pollegada* are still in use:—

1 *pollegada*	= 0.0275 *metro* (about 1 inch)
1 *pé* (12 *pollegadas*)	= 13 inches (about)
1 *vara* (40 *pollegadas*)	= 43·3 inches (3 ft. 7·3 in.)

WEIGHTS. *(Pesos.)*

English (Avoirdupois).	Portuguese.
1 ounce ...	= 28 *grammas*
1 lb. (16 oz.)	= 453 *grammas*
1 quarter (28 lb.)	= 12 *kilos.* 690 *grms.*
1 cwt. (112 lb.)	= 50 *kilos.* 750 *grms.*
1 ton (20 cwt.)	= 1015 *kilogrammas*

Portuguese.	English.
1 *gramma*	= 15·432 grains
1 *hectogramma*	= 3½ oz.
1 *kilogramma*	= 2·2 lb.
5 *kilos.*	= 11 lb.
1000 *kilos.*	= 19 cwt. 2 qr. 23 lb.

LIQUIDS. *(Liquidas.)*

English.	Portuguese.
1 pint	= ·57 *litro*
1 quart (2 pints)	= 1·14 *litros*
1 gallon (4 quarts)	= 4·45 ,,
1 barrel (36 gallons)	= 160·32 ,,
1 hogshead (54 gals.)	= 240·48 ,,

Portuguese.	English.
1 *litro*	= 1·76 pints; 0·22 gallon
5 *litros*	= 1 gallon 1 pint
1 *hectolitro*	= 22 gallons
1 *kilolitro*	= 220 gallons.

NOTE.—The Portuguese *almude* is still used. It varies in different towns; e.g., in Lisbon it equals 3·7 gals., in Oporto 5·6 gals.

NOTE.—The Portuguese weights still in use are as follows:—

1 *onça* ...	= 1 oz av. (about)
1 *arratel* (*libra*)	= 1·012 lb.
1 *arroba* ...	= 34·72 lb.
1 *quintal* ...	= 138·89 lb.
1 *tonelada* ...	= 1875 lb. (16 cwt. 83 lb.)

16 onças ...	= 1 *arratel* (or *libra*)
32 arrateis (libras)	= 1 *arroba*
4 arrobas ...	= 1 *quintal*
13½ quintaes ...	= 1 *tonelada.*

Postage.—The postage on LETTERS *from* Portugal *to* England, America and other countries is at the rate of 50 *reis* (2½d.) for 15 *grammas* (½ oz.), POST CARDS 20 *reis*, NEWSPAPERS 10 *reis* for every 50 *grammas*. The Portuguese *inland* rates on letters and post cards are *half* the above, on newspapers one quarter of the above.